Harry S. Truman

and the

Modern
American Presidency

Robert H. Ferrell

Harry S. Truman

and the

Modern
American Presidency

Edited by Oscar Handlin

HarperCollins*Publishers*

Library of Congress Cataloging in Publication Data

Ferrell, Robert H.
  Harry S. Truman and the modern American
presidency.

  (Library of American biography)
  Includes bibliographical references and index.
  1. Truman, Harry S., 1884–1972. 2. United States
—Politics and government—1945–1953. 3. Executive
power—United States. 4. Presidents—United States
—Biography. I. Title. II. Series.
E814.F47   1983   973.918'092'4 [B]   82-14889
ISBN 0-316-28123-9

LIBRARY OF CONGRESS CATALOG CARD NO. 82-14889

ISBN 0-673-39337-2

98 99 00 CRW 15 14 13 12 11 10

ALP

Printed in the United States of America

Editor's Preface

A trick of fate put the improbable Harry S. Truman into the White House at a crucial moment in the nation's history. The genius of American institutions and his own personality enabled him to meet the challenge.

Franklin Delano Roosevelt scarcely considered what would happen when the reins of power slipped from his own hands, and he gave little thought to who should succeed him. Earlier, political strategy had dictated his choice of John N. Garner and Henry Wallace as his candidates for the vice-presidency. Similar considerations of tactical availability guided the selection of his running mate in 1944.

The little-known senator from Missouri, whose political experience just a few years before had been limited to local county concerns, now stepped onto a worldwide stage. His responsibility was awesome. He had to bring to a successful conclusion the most devastating war in modern history. He had to guide American society to a peaceful demobilization, while at the same time confronting a ruthless antagonist, willing to sacrifice millions of lives in the pursuit of ideological goals. The president had to explain to a troubled people why the defeat of Germany and Japan had not assured the victory of freedom.

Truman also had to take the first steps toward modernizing the relationship of government to the economy. Memories of the terrible depression of the 1930s were still vivid, and Americans avidly sought to avoid a recurrence. In the process, they also wished to revise their assumptions about what a just social order should be; the unexpected president enunciated for them the social objectives of a fair deal for all elements in the nation's population. The United States would not attain those goals for decades more, but they received a memorable expression from Harry Truman.

Professor Ferrell's lively account traces the way in which a rural background, the experience of command in the First World War, and the realities of local politics prepared this president for his role. Drawing skillfully on Truman's own down-to-earth language, he creates a vivid portrait of a significant figure at a critical moment in American history.

OSCAR HANDLIN

Acknowledgments

I AM INDEBTED to many individuals, first of all General J. Lawton Collins, chief of staff of the U.S. Army during the Truman years, who kindly read the chapter on the Korean War. Former Secretary of Agriculture Charles F. Brannan read the explanation of the Brannan Plan. The staff of the Truman Library was helpful beyond measure—Benedict K. Zobrist, director; George Curtis, assistant director; Philip D. Lagerquist and Erwin J. Mueller, archivists par excellence; Elizabeth Safly, librarian, keeper of a vertical file that contains the most marvelous information; Pauline Testerman, photographic archivist. Every member of the library staff assisted in one way or another, including the two library interns in the summer of 1982, Christopher Boerner and Renee Voltmann. For reading of chapters I am indebted to Edward H. Buehrig, John Garry Clifford, Louis L. Gerson, Francis H. Heller, Richard L. Miller, Arnold A. Offner, William B. Pickett, William D. Tammeus, and John Edward Wilz. Karl O'Lessker shared his knowledge of politics of the time. Daniel F. Harrington allowed me to use his doctoral dissertation on the Berlin blockade. Ken Hechler offered information on the White House staff, of which he was a member. Marian and Joe Nixon furnished information on the president's later years. Judith Schaeffer, David Ershun, and Judith Ashkenaz of Total Concept Associates in Brattleboro, Vermont, handled the editing and production with aplomb. I am grateful to the staff of Little, Brown—Garret J. White, editor-in-chief, College Division; and to Susan Bowers, Sandy Manly, Mary E.

Tondorf-Dick, Nikki Sklare, and Julie Winston. Madelyn Leopold, former history editor, was very helpful. Oscar Handlin, editor of the Library of American Biography, thoroughly edited the manuscript better than any other series editor with whom I have dealt. And special thanks to Lila and Carolyn.

ROBERT H. FERRELL

Contents

Harry S. Truman
and the
Modern
American Presidency

Martha Ellen and John Anderson Truman, wedding day, December 28, 1881

I

Early Years

HARRY S. TRUMAN was born in a small, frame house in the village of Lamar, Missouri, on May 8, 1884. His mother's and his father's families had both come out west to Missouri from Kentucky. Although it is known that the Truman family originally was from England, the early genealogy is vague. The name presumably came from the Saxon "Tru man," and the family may have descended from William Truman, an English brewer prominent in the time of Cromwell. Truman beer was still being sold across the Atlantic during Truman's presidency, and occasionally someone would send the president an advertisement for the beer bearing the legend: "If it's Truman's it's best." Truman liked to tell his cousin Ethel Noland, the family genealogist, that the family descended from the beer baron.

Truman's parents, John Anderson Truman and Martha Ellen Truman, named him for his uncle, Harrison Young, using the diminutive, Harry. His middle initial was a compromise between the names of his two grandfathers, Solomon Young and Anderson Shipp Truman. Strictly speaking, therefore, the middle initial S stood for nothing, because it stood for both Solomon and Shipp. Grammarians later argued over whether to use a period after the initial, but the holder of the initial did not seem to care—if he was in a hurry, he left the period out, but when he thought about it he used it.

In Truman's early childhood, from 1884 to 1887, his family moved every year, from farm to farm. He later noticed that his first memory was of playing outside one of those farmhouses, chasing a frog around the yard, slapping his knees and laughing, while Grandmother Harriet Young laughed and laughed to see a two-year-old enjoying himself so much. Some of his other early memories included his mother dropping him from an upstairs window into the arms of Uncle Harrison, who had come to see the new baby in the household—Harry's brother Vivian—and, somewhat later, cries from an upstairs bedroom when his sister Mary Jane was born.

In 1887, during President Grover Cleveland's first term of office, the family moved to the farm of Uncle Harrison and Grandmother Young, where they remained for three years. In 1890 they moved to Independence, then a small town of several thousand people ten miles east of downtown Kansas City. Independence, the seat of Jackson County, had been founded by partisans of Andrew (Old Hickory) Jackson, while to the north Henry Clay's partisans founded adjoining Clay County, with Liberty as its county seat. In the 1830s the prophet Joseph Smith visited Independence and designated the area as a settlement for his followers. A plot of land near the courthouse was purchased as a place for a temple. The prophet later led his followers back to Illinois, where he died at the hands of a mob. His church survived, despite opposition from the then-heretical church of Brigham Young, as the Reorganized Church of Jesus Christ of Latter Day Saints; it established world headquarters in Independence. The town also became famous as the place from which the great Western trails began—to Santa Fe and to Oregon and California. Many years later, a namesake of Missouri's Senator Thomas Hart Benton painted a gigantic mural entitled "Independence and the Opening of the West" on the north wall of the main entrance of the Harry S. Truman Library. By that time Independence had grown to 60,000 inhabitants and was a suburb of Kansas City.

In Independence, the Truman family lived first in a house on Crysler Street, then in 1896 moved to West Waldo and River Boulevard, where they remained until 1902. There young Harry attended grade school and high school, graduating in 1901. A photograph was taken of his high school class of forty young men and women in front of a Victorian building that no longer exists. The building had a romanesque arched doorway and a stained-glass decoration with the legend, "Juventus Spes Mundi" ("Youth the Hope of the World"). The photograph showed the future president standing proudly in the back row, fourth from the left, a lad with round face and a shock of hair, in a carefully brushed suit, white shirt, and knotted tie. His spectacles caught the light of the occasion and circled his eyes— those eyes that, because of farsightedness, prevented him from applying to the United States Military Academy at West Point.

One of the young ladies smiling in that high school picture— at the far right in the second row—was Elizabeth Virginia (Bess) Wallace, aged sixteen, whom Harry had met eleven years earlier in Sunday school at the Presbyterian church. In grade school he had sat behind her and watched the little girl with the golden curls; as they grew older and went to high school, he oc- casionally talked with her and asked to carry her books. Because Harry's Cousin Nellie Noland, an expert Latinist, lived near 608 North Delaware Street, where Bess lived, Harry and Bess parsed their verbs and declined their nouns and adjectives with Cousin Nellie—when their "gang" on Delaware Street was not playing together or taking hay rides and engaging in other young people's activities of the era. Harry's boyhood was a pleasant one among friends in the small town, friends who remained in touch for the rest of their lives. The valedictorian of his class was Charles G. (Charlie) Ross, later a reporter for the St. Louis *Post-Dispatch*, who won the Pulitzer Prize for journalism and even- tually served as President Truman's press secretary.

With his high school graduation, Harry's idyll in Indepen- dence came to an end. His father had engaged in grain specula- tions in Kansas City that turned out badly, and the family lost the house on Waldo Street and moved to Kansas City. At this point in his life, there could be no hope of college for Harry. He and his brother Vivian went to work in a Kansas City bank as clerks, and their father found employment in a grain elevator.

Young Harry started at the National Bank of Commerce at
Tenth and Walnut at thirty-five dollars a month. For a while he
lived with his parents, but when they moved away he lived with
Aunt Emma Colgan, and then in a boarding house, paying five
dollars a week for room, breakfast and dinner and an additional
ten cents a day for a box lunch. One of his fellow roomers in the
boarding house was a young bank clerk from Abilene, Kansas,
named Arthur Eisenhower, a brother of a future president.

Truman's work at the Commerce Bank was not fascinating, if
only because of the personality of the bank's vice-president,
Charles H. Moore, whose job it was to hire and fire. According
to Truman, Moore could have humiliated the nerviest man in
the world and was "never so happy as when he could call some
poor inoffensive little clerk up before him in the grand lobby of
the biggest bank west of the Mississippi and tell him how dumb
and inefficient he was because he'd sent a check belonging to the
State Bank of Oakland, Kansas, to Ogden, Utah." The bank was
owned by Dr. W. S. Woods, who had been a country doctor at
Fulton, Missouri. Woods had gone from medicine to finance
and eventually became owner of the Commerce, where he
counted pennies and nickels and made a fortune. Because of his
dislike of these two men, Truman changed jobs in 1905, moving
to the Union National Bank, where he soon began to earn one
hundred dollars a month, a magnificent salary at that time.

During Truman's years at the Commerce and the Union
National, he seized the opportunity for what was known in those
days, without embarrassment, as culture. Numerous vaudeville
greats came to Kansas City—the Four Cohans, including George
M., and such attractions as Chauncey Olcott, the famous actress
Sarah Bernhardt, Marguerita Sylva, Eddie Foy, "Chic" Sale, and
others. On stage, Harry saw Richard Mansfield in "Dr. Jekyll
and Mr. Hyde," which so frightened him that he was afraid to go
home after seeing it. He also saw Walker Whiteside in "Richard
III," Sir Henry Irving and Ellen Terry in "The Merchant of
Venice," "Julius Caesar," and "Hamlet," and a local stock
company that performed Shakespeare at the Auditorium. Tru-

man ushered at one of the theaters and so managed to see many of the performances for nothing.

Then there was the music. When the Metropolitan Opera came to Convention Hall, Truman saw "Parsifal," "Lohengrin," "Cavalleria Rusticana," "Pagliacci," and "Les Huguenots." He paid his way to hear Joseph Lhevinne and Ignaz Jan Paderewski and ever afterward remembered their playing. Later, he often described how Paderewski had taught him to play "Minuet in G." Truman had studied the piano when he was in high school, before his father's financial collapse had brought the lessons to a sudden end.

In 1906, Harry Truman's Uncle Harrison, who wished to retire, proposed that John and Martha Ellen Truman take over Grandmother Young's big farm near Grandview. When their parents moved back to the farm, Harry and Vivian moved back too, both quitting their bank jobs. From 1906 until 1917, Harry farmed the full section of land, 640 acres, belonging to Grandmother Young. When she died in 1909, the land was willed to the Truman family and to Uncle Harrison, and when the uncle died in 1916, his share went to Harry's mother. Harry's father had died in 1914, from a strangulated hernia suffered when he lifted too large a load in his part-time job as road overseer. Harry then did the farming himself, with whatever hired hands he could engage. Meanwhile, Vivian returned to work in Kansas City.

Running a big farm was an enormous task in the era before tractors; each day it was necessary to get the horses out to do the work and to care for the horses when they were not working. There was a continual round of chores, including repair of machinery. Although the stationery of the firm read "J. A. Truman & Son," Harry Truman was essentially the proprietor. He raised Black Angus cattle, and he rotated crops at a time when many American farmers were content to mine the soil year after year. Growing wheat, corn, oats, and clover, with the clover sown in rotation so as to rest the land, occupied Truman's hours from morning to night. About 1910 a visitor to the farm snapped a photograph of Harry S. Truman behind a team of horses, sitting high on a single-row cultivator and going down through a field of corn some weeks before the Fourth of July—when, according to farm lore, a good field should be knee-high. In the distance lay nothing but horizon above the bleak, rich flatland that gladdened the hearts of Midwestern farmers. This land, properly drained and with crops rotated, produced bumper crops year after year.

Truman's preparation for the presidency began with his early life on the farm, the kind of experience that many a lad in the years before and just after the turn of the twentieth century never forgot. In later years, when people began moving to the cities or the suburbs, the value of farm experience seemed more and more remote. After 1950 it no longer was important for politicians to boast that they had been born and raised on a farm. For Truman, however, the farm was the essential beginning.

In the mornings the sun came up suddenly in the farmland of western Missouri, rising over the horizon in a few seconds and flooding fields with brightness. Farmers were already out with their teams, ready to use all the daylight to work until, in the evening, the long shadows stretched out so that one could no longer see the corn rows or the lines of cut hay. It was a hard life, measured out in intervals of twenty or twenty-five minutes, after each of which it was necessary to rest the horses, then start down another row, riding jerkily as the plow or cultivator bumped along, and watching to keep a straight line, watching to see that both horses moved together, pulling equally on the load. Sometimes Truman would see the clouds darken and fill up and then, just a mile or two away, the heavens would open, and down would come sheets of rain, while on his own field there was just a sprinkle or two or perhaps even sunshine.

The farm was not Truman's sole interest, however. On those strange rain-and-sun days in 1912, between cultivator runs, he periodically walked over to the telegraph office at nearby Grandview to get news of the Democratic national convention in Baltimore, where the forces of Champ Clark, speaker of the house of representatives, a local Missouri politician supported by Harry's father John, battled the rising forces of Governor Woodrow Wilson of New Jersey. The young Missouri farmer was delighted when Wilson won.

With a partner, Truman invested in a zinc and lead mine in Oklahoma. The venture failed, with a loss of $2,000. If he and his partner had had enough money to take a rig into the area, they would have become rich. He also invested in oil leases in Texas, Oklahoma, and Kansas. Early in 1917, he and two partners had a well drilled 900 feet on a 320-acre lease in Eureka, Kansas, but Truman gave it up when he joined the army, and the partners let the lease go. The well was right on top of the famous Teter Pool; had Truman stayed home and run his oil company, he probably would have become a millionaire.

All the while he was busy with Masonry, a widespread and celebrated secret society for fraternal purposes that traced back to medieval times. Its principles had attracted him when his cousin came to Grandview and told him about them in 1909. Truman joined the lodge in nearby Belton that year, and, after following around a leader of the grand lodge who was going from lodge to lodge teaching the ritual, in 1910 Harry obtained a dispensation for a lodge in Grandview and was appointed presiding officer. He then became the master and maintained his membership and interest in Freemasonry for the rest of his life. In 1930 he was started in the grand lodge line of the Masons of Missouri and was elected grand master in 1940. This interest thus antedated his appearance on the political scene by many years. During his time on the farm he found Masonry fascinating and later remarked that he had learned the ritual by reciting it to the plow horses.

A third and most important occupation of Truman's farming years was his courtship of Bess Wallace. The friendship of the two high school chums had lapsed, perhaps because young Truman had moved to Kansas City and was working in the banks and ushering in the theater. When he moved back to the farm, there was much work to do, and it was no easy task to ride by train and streetcar, via a circuitous route, the dozen or so miles from Grandview to Independence. The trains and cars were often late when he visited Aunt Ella Noland and her daughters, Ethel and Nellie. He often spent the night in their parlor, sleeping on the couch. By this time the Nolands had moved to a little house right across the street from 219 North Delaware, where Bess then lived. One day he came into his aunt's kitchen to learn that Mrs. Wallace, Bess's mother, had sent over a cake and that the plate needed to be returned. As Truman's daughter Margaret remembered the incident many years later from family talk, her father seized the plate "with something approaching the speed of light," walked across to the Wallace house, and rang the doorbell. Bess answered the door, and the courtship was on. By early 1917, Harry and Bess were engaged.

In April 1917, when Truman was almost thirty-three years old, his bucolic life—courting his boyhood sweetheart, farming, and pursuing his interests in zinc, lead, and oil—suddenly ended. The United States was entering the First World War. President Wilson went before Congress on April 2 and asked for a declaration of war; he got it four days later. Truman and his countrymen had taken little interest in the events that led up to the declaration. In 1916 Wilson had warned the Germans that, if they again pursued a policy of "unrestricted" submarine warfare—by which he meant the sinking of American ships on sight, without provision for the safety of passengers and crew, or the sinking of foreign passenger liners in which American lives were lost—he would break diplomatic relations and presumably would follow with a declaration of war. The German government did not fear American retaliation; the army of the United States was about the size of Portugal's. The British had already penned up the German High Seas Fleet, and the Germans hoped to starve the British isles by cutting off Argentine and Australian grain; they calculated that the American reaction would not affect the outcome. The German decision was made early in January; the United States acted in early April.

These events almost immediately put Truman into the army. In 1905, at the age of twenty-one, he had joined the National Guard and was a member for several years. He attended drills and summer camp regularly, until he found his duties on the farm too time-consuming. When President Wilson called out the guard during the Mexican crisis of 1916, he was unable to go. When the president again called up the guard in 1917, however, Truman went to work filling out his field artillery battery and helping to enlarge it into a regiment. He devoted such effort to bringing in enlistments that he told his fellow workers he thought he deserved to be a sergeant, whereupon, and much to his surprise, he was made a first lieutenant.

When the war began, Lieutenant Truman soon was off to Camp Doniphan in Oklahoma, just west of and adjoining Fort Sill. There, among other duties, he supervised the regimental canteen, together with Sergeant Eddie Jacobson, whom he had known years earlier when he had worked in the Commerce Bank. Drawing on Eddie's experience as a men's furnishings buyer, he and Truman collected two dollars from each of the 1100 men in their artillery regiment, went to Oklahoma City, and bought items for the canteen that the army did not furnish. They sold the items at a modest profit, which they eventually returned to the men. The fame of the canteen spread, and men from other units hastened to buy, adding to the profit of the canteen. Its success was due to careful buying and accounting, and also to such precautions as substituting cash registers for the typical cigar boxes.

On March 30, 1918, the day before Easter Sunday, Truman and an advance contingent of the 129th Field Artillery Regiment sailed for France aboard the *George Washington*, the same vessel that some months later took President Wilson to France to attend the peace conference. The ship docked at Brest on April 13. A few days later, Truman went to Montigny-sur-Aube to artillery school to learn how to shoot the famous French 75, the principal allied artillery piece during World War I. In April 1918 he was promoted to captain.

Everything seemed routine until July, when he was given command of Battery D, the most unruly in the regiment. Truman later wrote that this group of spirited Irishmen and German Catholics from Kansas City had broken four commanders. He had been badly frightened several times in his life, he would recall, and that morning when he first faced "the boys" of the battery was one of them. He called together the corporals and sergeants and told them forthrightly that it was their job to get along with him, not him with them. He told them that, if any of them couldn't do it, they should let him know at once and he would "bust them back right now." Everyone was left with the feeling that the new captain was in control.

"We got along," he remembered; but it was much better than that. The men of Battery D idolized their captain, referring to "Captain Harry" for the rest of their lives. In the Truman Library at Independence are hundreds of letters to the captain, many in longhand, relating births of children and grandchildren, deaths of wives, humdrum and extraordinary activities. Many of the letters came from Kansas City and environs, but quite a few were from remote localities. As the decades passed, the letters came from Arizona and California, where the old veterans found the climate more attractive. For every letter that came in, a letter went back, usually typed but often with a longhand addition to give it a familiar touch. Many years later, one man wrote about the time he and Captain Harry had sat in a half-ruined French house and watched the fire burning in the fireplace, the flames dancing. The man had mentioned at the time that his father once told him a fire had a soul, and Captain Harry had gravely agreed. In his letter, the veteran wrote that he was about to go back to France to see the battlefields, and Truman replied emotionally that he, too, had thought of such a trip. He asked his friend to please send postcards of the places of long ago.

Not all Truman's wartime experiences involved sitting in front of a fireplace; the later famous Battle of Who Run was a small but potentially deadly engagement in which the Americans fired several hundred rounds of gas shells at the Germans, who responded with an artillery barrage over Truman's battery. His troops suddenly had the dangerous task of bringing up the horses, hitching them to the guns, and getting the guns out of there before the Germans blew them up. In the midst of the chaos, one of the sergeants yelled, "Run boys, they've got a bracket on us!" The men began to scatter, but the captain, instantly on the scene, with his eyes blazing, shouted at the cannoneers to return and do their duty. He used every expression he could think of, which was quite a few. They soon came back and hitched the horses. Despite the rain of shells, the explosions, and the clods of dirt heaving in all directions, laced with deadly metal from the shrapnel, they got the guns out of there.

The war moved along toward its end, although not without moments of false hope. On October 27, 1918, Battery D was moving down a road when the French edition of the New York *Herald* was distributed, announcing in black-letter headlines that an armistice was on. Just then a German 150 shell burst to the right of the road and another to the left. One of the sergeants remarked, "Captain, those G.D. Germans haven't seen this paper." From the captain came a wry smile.

Some days later, the guns fell silent at last, and on Easter Sunday, April 9, 1919, the former German ship *Zeppelin*, a rough rider, steamed into New York harbor with Captain Truman and his men aboard. "I'd been gone from that city just a year and twenty days," he wrote more than a quarter-century later. "I made a resolution that if old lady Liberty in New York harbor wanted to see me again she'd have to turn around." After a long rail trip to Camp Funston in Kansas, and discharge on May 6, the war was over for Truman.

The war was a turning point in Truman's life in that it took him away from the farm forever. Not long after his return, he arranged to sell his farm implements and moved into Independence, where he married Bess on June 28, 1919, the very day the Treaty of Versailles was signed. After a short wedding trip to Chicago, Detroit, and Port Huron, Michigan, they moved into the house where Bess had lived with her mother, at 219 North Delaware. Truman's mother and sister, Mary Jane, remained in the farmhouse near Grandview until 1940, when the farm was foreclosed, whereupon they moved into a little bungalow in the town. In this regard, Truman's life was no different from the lives of millions of other Americans who left the farm in the postwar years, partly because of the fall in farm prices in the 1920s but also because the life of loneliness and intensely hard work had become irksome once war revealed the attractions of comradeship and travel. The heady war experience made it impossible to go back to the farm. Truman's two years in the army had also brought a realization that he had a way with his fellows—that his was a very attractive personality, to which the men of the battery had responded with enthusiasm. He did not sense in any grand way that his leadership could accomplish great things, not only with a battery but with the politics of Jackson County, Missouri, the United States Senate, and the presidency of the United States. But he dimly realized that comradeship and leadership pointed to new and interesting activities.

The initial result of Truman's army experience was the Kansas City haberdashery of Truman and Jacobson, which originated, of course, from experience with the army canteen. After careful planning, Harry Truman and Eddie Jacobson decided to open a store. They obtained a five-year lease on a location on Twelfth Street, near the Muehlebach Hotel, and opened for business in the autumn of 1919. For a while they did a remarkable trade, not merely with returned veterans of their own and other organizations but with passersby who had money to buy fairly expensive shirts and ties and hats. Then came indications of a national business recession—the sort that followed every war in the history of the United States except World War II. Truman and Jacobson were caught in the recession of 1921–1922. Ignoring the signs and refusing to sell out when they could have made a deal that would have returned their investment, they had held their shelf stock while prices plummeted. When they finally closed the store, they had lost at least $25,000. The loss was in the form of several large bank notes, not all of which were covered by collateral. There was also the long lease on the store, which the holder refused to negotiate. After a tedious and embarrassing renegotiation of whatever was possible, the partners went their separate ways and tried to pay off their debts over the years. By 1925 finances were so pressing that Eddie Jacobson declared bankruptcy. Truman narrowly avoided it and continued to pay off his debts, slowly but surely. For twenty years after the closure in 1922, he was strapped for money. When the family farm was threatened by foreclosure in 1940, he could not raise the three or four thousand dollars necessary to keep it, although it had been in the Truman and Young families for a century. The tragedy was compounded when his aging mother, who was forced to move, slipped on the stairs and broke her hip while trying to get about in a strange house.

In 1922, however, these problems were yet to evolve. The "busted merchant," as he once described himself, consoled himself that he had made a wonderfully happy marriage to the girl he had loved since 1890, that he had enormously benefited from the army experience, which had widened his horizons, that the farm years had not been idyllic but had given him a sense of resolution and a feeling for the verities of life, and that his four years in the banks had shown him something of finance and much more of culture in a large metropolis.

The wedding party, June 28, 1919; l. to r., Helen Wallace (Mrs. Truman's cousin), best man Theodore Marks (former Captain, Battery "C", 129th Field Artillery), the groom, Frank Wallace (Mrs. Truman's brother), the bride, and Louise Wells (Mrs. Truman's cousin)

II

From Jackson County
to Washington

THE EARLY YEARS of a future president of the United States should contain a wealth of experience, a series of small events or circumstances that point to larger matters, providing opportunities to focus the mind or energies or ambition. As years pass, there is an upward movement or a simple accumulation of judgment that makes higher calculations possible. All the while, the future great man must keep perspective, understanding the people and traditions from which he comes and learning to appreciate not merely his immediate family and remote relatives but people far away.

Harry Truman had not been through any such testing by 1922, when he first ran for public office. There had been no progression, no upward movement, just a group of experiences that only later appeared to have a pattern. During his presidency and in retirement, Truman told visitors that a man needed three experiences to get ahead in government: the farm, finance, and the army. He had all three, but he had not planned his life that way. A more accurate account of his early years would have stressed their episodic nature—his trying this and that and no serious or obvious straightening of his life by 1922, when he was only two years from the halfway point of life for people of our century, the age of forty. Neither Harry nor Bess would have seen signs of success in 1922. They might have anticipated opportunities, but they would have considered them late in coming.

In respect to the larger currents of economy, ideas, or even politics in the year 1922, Truman had not gone far. He knew little about the great economic changes of the decades that preceded him—that the United States of the rural past had begun to disappear in the 1850s and that the growth of industry and cities marked every decade thereafter, especially the 1880s and 1890s and the turn of the century. He had spent his early youth in a small town, then four years in Kansas City, then eleven years on the farm, where things had not changed much from the way they were during the Civil War, when Grandmother Young tried to keep the place going and keep Yankee soldiers away from the hogs (she failed). Truman understood little of finance beyond passing cancelled checks from one village bank to another; his experience had been in the basement of the Commerce Bank, not upstairs with the nervy vice-president. The economics of Kansas City, not to mention the state of Missouri, the United States, and the world, was all foreign to him. He had taken part in the speculation of the time, investing in zinc and lead and oil, but nothing had happened, either from ill luck or from lack of knowledge.

Truman also seemed not to know much about the ideas of the period before and after the Great War. He did not read deeply, and perhaps not at all. When he was growing up in Independence and could not take part in childhood games because of his eyes, he had gone to the library; he later said that he read all the books, including encyclopedias, in addition to reading the Bible at home. He must have overstated. In later years at the bank, on the farm, in the army, and at the haberdashery, he surely had little time to read.

As for major political problems—the problems with government in the United States after World War I—Truman knew little about them. The war brought into focus the insufficiencies of preceding years, the inability of local and state government to deal with economic and social change. People needed protection against abuses by their contemporaries, and as people moved into cities it was necessary to make rules. The country was being brought together by streetcars and automobiles as well as railroads, and regional differences were diminishing. Small government meant trouble. Not always in an understanding way, the presidential administrations of Theodore Roosevelt, William H. Taft, and Woodrow Wilson sought to make rules, but rules defined the interstices of individual advantage. American politics was entering a new era in the early 1920s, and Truman dimly sensed the fact. Only a chance encounter with an army friend took him into politics.

A grounding in a profession, and Truman always considered politics a profession, is important, however late it may be, and it afterward became clear that Truman's move into county politics in 1922 marked an end to disorder in his life, a closing of the period in which he merely went from task to task. From that point on, his life was politics, experience after experience, with all the order and progression it had lacked. By the time he reached the presidency, he knew the ways of local, state, and national politics. He did not plan his life that way—perhaps no one plans his or her life—but he could not have done better if he had planned.

As president, Truman never had any use for would-be politicians who did not start at the bottom. He believed no lucky breaks made up for ringing doorbells on the precinct level and speaking in all the little halls and fraternal assembly places and church basements. In Jackson County, a would-be politician had to placate minor political factions and leaders without toadying to them. He also had to get along with, without being dominated by, a big-city leader with statewide and even national ambitions, Tom Pendergast of Kansas City.

Truman's decision to go into county politics stemmed from his army experiences. In 1917–1919 he had become acquainted with James Pendergast, a young lieutenant in his regiment whose father, Mike, was the younger brother of Boss Tom. One afternoon in the spring of 1922, when the haberdashery was

failing and Truman was in a quandary over what to do, Jim
Pendergast and his father happened into the store and urged the
former captain to run for eastern judge of Jackson County. The
county commissioners were known as judges, and there were
three—one elected from Independence and environs, the rural
eastern part of the county, and another from the western part,
Kansas City. The third was elected at large and known as the
presiding judge. Truman would be able to get the votes of
numerous veterans, of course, and he had relatives in every
township. He had spent his life there, and was not considered a
"foreigner." He even had occupied a petty county office. After
his father had been injured while working as road overseer,
Harry had taken over the task of repairing the township roads.
As a reward, he was given the postmastership of Grandview, a
job he passed on to a widow who needed the money.

Truman considered the Pendergasts' proposal and, after a
personal survey of his prospects, he decided to make the race.
He knew that the imminent closing of the store would put him
out of a job anyway. Because the county was traditionally
Democratic, the election that counted was the primary, and he
therefore began to collect promises among his possible supporters. His first experiences of running for office were ex-
cruciating. An embarrassed Truman almost muffed his initial
opportunity to speak at a political rally. He sat on the stage of a
now-forgotten hall, hands shaking, knees knocking, as candidates stood up, one after another, and made statements about
what was right about their candidacies and what was wrong
about their predecessors. His turn came, and his mind turned
blank—he could think of nothing. He managed to stand, move
to the small lectern, look at his staring audience, and blurt out
that he hoped they would support him in the primary, whereupon he sat down to a patter of applause. Later, the speeches
came more easily but were not memorable, for Truman in those
years was a poor public speaker, his flat Missouri voice easily
turning to monotone. His army supporters laced the audiences,

however, and made up in enthusiasm for what the candidate lacked in oratory, and the result was all right.

In August he received the Democratic nomination, and in November he was elected. He was sworn in on January 1, 1923. When he sat down in one of the big chairs behind the high bench in the courthouse office in Independence, Truman began his political education. He was to spend ten years on the court, two as eastern judge and eight as presiding judge.

When Judge Truman took the oath in January 1923, he had to learn about the law and his duties. The main task was to care for county roads, including gullies and mudholes and bridges, a serious problem in a large, growing metropolitan area. Another task was the management of the county home for the indigent aged.

The work of the court was complicated enough, but the politics surrounding it was extraordinary. Anyone who failed to calculate who was important and where support was coming from could not last in the swirl of Jackson County politics, which had a large admixture of the Irish saloonkeeper–hotel proprietor activity of the Pendergast brothers, Tom and Mike, and of the factionalism of the Jackson era, when Old Hickory's supporters organized the county in opposition to the Clay county to the north. When Truman ran for eastern judge, he did not have to do much calculation of political forces. The two principal Democratic factions, those of the Pendergast brothers and of another local boss, Joseph B. Shannon, united to support him against the incumbent James Compton, a local Independence real estate man. The governor had appointed Compton, and he did not have much local influence. The Pendergast-Shannon cooperation was mainly against the presiding judge, Miles Bulger, who used road contracts and others to enrich himself and, more to the point, was trying to form a rival organization of his own. Truman was part of the effort to get him out. After the election, with Bulger deposed, matters became more complicated, for Shannon and the Pendergasts soon were after the substantial patronage associated with the county court. Allotting jobs meant not merely prying out Bulger appointees and satisfying the victorious factions but also getting the new appointees to do the work. In the latter task, Judges Truman, H. F. McElroy, and Elihu Hayes had the ardent support of Boss Tom, who told them to fire any man who did not do the job.

As Truman remembered it years later, the court was always in a fuss about something, and one of its fusses resulted in Truman's defeat for reelection in 1924. Judge Hayes, who represented the Shannon faction, known as the Rabbits, was after jobs that Judge McElroy wanted for the Pendergast faction, known as the Goats. Truman naturally voted with the Goats, since his entry into politics had been through Jim Pendergast. As a result, Shannon took offense and in 1924 put up another man for Truman's job. The Republicans put up a harness worker. (A quarter-century earlier, when Truman lived on Crysler Street, this same harness maker had produced a contraption by which a real goat pulled the wagon of Harry and his brother Vivian.) The harness maker won the election, the only time in Truman's political career when he was defeated for office. For the next year and a half, until the primary in 1926, Truman enrolled as a salesman for memberships in the Kansas City Automobile Club, put on a whirlwind campaign, and made a good living at it.

In 1926 Truman filed his candidacy for presiding judge, somewhat against the wishes of Mike Pendergast, who thought he should have filed for county collector, a job that paid $25,000 a year because it was conducted on a percentage basis. Truman wanted the collectorship, which would have taken care of his debts, but Tom Pendergast decided, because Truman was familiar with the county court, to give the collector's job to another politician. That autumn, Truman won the presiding judgeship with a majority of 16,000 votes. He held the office until he went to the United States Senate in 1935.

There was a great deal of work for the presiding judge. Truman decided that Jackson County needed a modern administration, not the self-serving, time-serving officialdom of the past. In the 1920s there was a great deal of highway construction throughout the United States, and Truman became a well-known member of the National Old Trails Association. He sensed that there could be enormous economic development if the county constructed roads properly. It was also necessary to get rid of the expensive "pie crusts" (lightly cemented roads) built by the Bulger administration. For constructing new roads, building a skyscraper courthouse in Kansas City, and re-modeling the courthouse in Independence, Judge Truman floated two bond issues, one in 1928 for $6.5 million and one in 1931 for $7.9 million. Contracts always went to the low bidder, and a bipartisan pair of assistants chosen for absolute honesty carefully surveyed the county's needs. Citizens voted for both bond issues in overwhelmingly favorable majorities, at a time when similar bond issues for Kansas City alone failed because of well-founded suspicion of graft, a practice by which some politicians make personal profit from public funds. As presiding judge, Truman gave Jackson County one of the most notable administrations in the entire United States.

Judge Truman decided that a modern county management had to be without graft; making sufficient money available for new roads meant that there was not enough for graft. Furthermore, graft was dishonest, and Truman always had been honest. He knew that it was necessary to allot patronage jobs to please the political factions, but he always drew the line between patronage and graft, willing to help with the former but not with the latter. In dealing with his two fellow judges, he often resorted to trickery, having observed that they "used to shoot craps while court was in session down behind the bench while I transacted the business. . . . when I wanted something done I'd let Barr and Vrooman start a crap game and then introduce a long and technical order. Neither of them would have time to read it and over it would go. I got a lot of good legislation for Jackson County over while they shot craps." Even then, compromise was necessary, and, although he was not responsible, $1 million in general revenue slipped away to the grafters—a price, Truman uneasily calculated, that was necessary to keep their hands off the road bond issues. Although he was presiding judge, Truman had only one vote on the three-man county court.

In the effort to modernize county administration, Truman found an unexpected ally in Boss Tom Pendergast, who, Truman understood, had his roots in the city's poorest wards and performed many necessary functions. In the days before poor relief, the political boss doled out groceries. If someone needed to be buried, the boss made the arrangements. If necessary, the boss provided jobs. Precinct, ward, and city machines ran on the exchanges of votes for jobs, known as patronage; it was the glue that held machines together. Patronage employees kicked back part of their pay to the boss or to the boss's organization. The boss did larger favors for businessmen and companies desiring franchises or legislation or simple legal transactions that could prove difficult without the boss's cooperation. Payment for these larger favors also went into the boss's personal or organizational coffers. In the nineteenth century a boss frequently used brute force and got out the votes any way he could—by providing alcohol, outright purchase, or falsification by having voting repeaters use the names of people who had moved away or died. In the twentieth century with the Australian, or secret ballot, voting became more honest, but repeaters still often came out in force. The boss's precinct and ward men, known as ward heelers, often used more repeaters than necessary, because a big vote showed their hard work.

Boss Tom Pendergast was a short, red-faced, barrel-chested man with huge hands that, earlier in his career, might have closed on some uncooperative Irish or Italian throat. A dozen years before Truman met him, the boss had inherited his wards from his brother and gained control of the city. By the time Truman became associated with him, Boss Tom had tamed down, and his former strongarm approaches were no longer necessary. He had helped to elect a United States senator, James A. Reed, the Democratic nemesis of President Wilson who hated the League of Nations and blacks equally and believed that the

League was a plot to elevate blacks. The boss presided over Kansas City from a dingy office that became the best-known local address, a place where politicians waited in the anteroom to take their democratic turns, saying whatever was necessary to the boss, who then decided what was necessary. Tom Pendergast lived in a $115,000 mansion that belied his primitive beginnings, and he was head of a well-ordered family, which attended Mass each Sunday. For their summer vacations, the boss and his wife went to Europe aboard the best transatlantic liners and enjoyed the cuisine, scenery, and the leisures of the Continent for the moment before the boss plunged back into the politics of his city.

Pendergast was an old-time political boss—moral in his own way, very shrewd, and utterly reliable if he gave his word. He ran a machine, of course, and his lieutenants, in their enthusiasm, voted absentees and dead people. The boss also sold cement, and everyone in Kansas City and eventually throughout Missouri bought from his Ready-Mixed Concrete Company. His influence in Kansas City was more benign than malign, however, until, in the 1930s, a racketeer named Johnny Lazia became one of his lieutenants and welcomed criminals to Kansas City, where Lazia controlled the police department. A gunman's bullet soon ended Lazia's life, and the city quieted down. In the mid-1930s, however, Boss Tom became ill, lost his judgment, and at the same time began playing the horses. He required large sums of money, which insurance companies gave him so that they could obtain favorable rulings from the state's insurance commissioner, whom Boss Tom controlled. He failed to report this money, $750,000, on his income tax. Indeed, he had submitted incomplete tax returns since 1927.

In county politics, Boss Tom needed a suitable ally in the east, and when ill health prevented his brother Mike from acting as his deputy there, Judge Truman stepped into the role, honest yet cooperative. Truman realized that, if he wanted to be in politics in Jackson County, he would have to have some sort of relations with Boss Tom. He understood that a political organization required patronage. He did not, however, agree to kickbacks or outside graft from selling favors, drawing a line between patronage and graft. Truman had his roots in the rural eastern part of Jackson County and could deliver the vote for programs he favored, and Pendergast could deliver the Kansas City vote. Together they could dominate the county court, with its large patronage potential. It was the sort of local political alliance that worked, and worked well, and both men appreciated its meaning for government of the county and city. Pendergast did not force Truman, as presiding judge, to do anything he considered unethical. At the outset, the boss asked to bring around some friends—contractors who were concerned that they would get no business under the closed-bidding arrangements sponsored by Truman. The group met, and Boss Tom told his friends to state their case. Then Truman stated his case, which was that bids went to the lowest bidder, whereupon Boss Tom told the contractors to "get out of here" because the presiding judge was a contrary Missourian. After they left, Pendergast said to Truman, "You carry out your commitments to the voters." The boss did not often give his word about something, but when he did it was worth its weight in gold. Truman liked Boss Tom for that—a way of behaving, he later noticed, different from that of many politicians with whom he had to do business.

As the years passed and the golden 1920s came to an end, the presiding judge of Jackson County felt new pressures against the county budget. In the 1920s the problems had been the grafters and the need for roads; in the early 1930s men wanted to work and looked to the county for help. Stating the problem so simply, of course, hardly conveys the misery, the confusion, and the dashed hopes that accompanied the Great Depression, when economic cataclysm befell the entire Western world in the years after 1929.

The causes of the crash were too far from Truman's local experience, and he could only sense them. The speculation of the era, the buying of stocks and bonds, was beyond his financial ability, for he was trying desperately to juggle his personal finances and eventually pay off the debt of the haberdashery. He was unaware of the depression's more remote causes: they were in part the economic derangements brought on by World War I, the changing of economies to war production, thereby creating (especially in Europe) such new industries as steel, shipbuilding, and chemicals, which did not disappear in the 1920s but often were protected by tariffs. Everything kited along during the 1920s, especially the payment of German reparations, which was accomplished by loans from the United States to enable the German government to pay Britain and France, so that they in turn could pay their war debts to the United States—a fantastic circle of payments. Behind all the uneconomic arrangements were larger changes in the world's economies: loss of industrial leadership by Great Britain because of competition from Germany and the United States, shifting patterns of national development that were disguised by shipping fees, investment dividends, and the panoply of empire. The world's industrial arrangements became intertwined, and the structures needed constant transmission of funds from one nation to the other. Theoretically, the marketplace made the adjustments, but tariffs and manipulation prevented adjustments. The so-called world economy became, rather, a group of national economies glued together by such rickety payments as reparations and war debts. Stock market speculation in the United States had attracted money from all over the world, and when the market broke in October 1929, it was the end. In subsequent months, by a ripple effect, disaster spread everywhere.

Truman did not understand the larger movements of goods and services, prices and dividends, but he did see the abysmal results in Jackson County: loss of jobs, falling prices, unpaid taxes, crowding in the county poorhouse, and querulous inquiries to the county's presiding judge as to what he was going to do about people's needs. In 1930 things got worse. From the faraway government of President Herbert Hoover came reassurance that it was all a short-run readjustment, as in 1921–1922, but Judge Truman did not appreciate this philosophy.

There was talk about turning the corner, and President Hoover summoned national leaders to a series of conferences to decide what to do. The conferences accomplished nothing; in 1931 farm foreclosures increased, and in 1932 stark tragedy was everywhere.

When President Franklin D. Roosevelt took office in March 1933 the Great Depression was at its worst, and Judge Truman had done his best to give county jobs to the needy and to keep Jackson County going. Money became available from Washington almost at once, and Boss Tom arranged for Truman to take charge of relief in the state of Missouri. Truman met with the federal relief administrator, Harry Hopkins, and worked through him to distribute federal funds locally. He did this in addition to his regular duties in Jackson County.

The depression did not end in 1933 nor in 1934, Truman's last year as presiding judge. It went on until the country entered World War II after the Pearl Harbor attack in 1941. Jobs were scarce throughout the 1930s. During that decade, Truman slowly pulled himself out of debt, paying off the costs of the haberdashery. At one point, when a note held by a Kansas City bank was taken over by another bank and the second bank failed, the note went up at public auction. Vivian Truman bought it at a low price and Harry paid Vivian. Throughout the 1930s, however, Truman was paying his debts and was pressed for funds.

Meanwhile, Truman's life took a new and interesting turn. In 1934 he reached his fiftieth birthday. His work with the county was coming to an end, for he could not continue in office indefinitely; the principle of passing jobs on was never far from the minds of local Democratic politicos in Missouri. Times were difficult during the Great Depression, and Truman looked for some refuge in which he could continue for the rest of his life. He had hoped that the refuge might be the United States House of Representatives. In 1932 a reapportionment of representatives to Missouri had forced a redistricting, and Truman had helped fix the new boundaries so that Jackson County obtained two seats. The new Fourth District, almost the entire county outside Kansas City, was made to order for his own election. Unfortunately, Tom Pendergast for some reason endorsed Judge C. Jasper Bell, and it appeared to be time for Truman to get out of politics and go back to the farm. Then the Democratic senator from Missouri, Bennett Champ Clark, son of the Speaker of the House of Representatives who fought Wilson at Baltimore in 1912, sought to extend his power by dictating selection of a senator from the western part of the state. Tradition allotted each metropolis one seat. Now Clark, who was from St. Louis, wanted the Kansas City senator as his rubber stamp. Boss Tom was not about to let Bennett Clark overreach himself; after several other candidates proved unavailable, he nominated Harry S. Truman for the office.

The primary of 1934 was a tough one, but Truman took Kansas City and the rural counties and won the primary by a 40,000-vote plurality. On January 30, 1935, he proudly took office as junior senator from the state of Missouri. Bennett Clark, maybe with inner reluctance, led him down the aisle to the podium, where the vice-president of the United States, John N. Garner, administered the oath.

Truman came to know Cactus Jack Garner intimately and much enjoyed his company, although he privately admitted that Garner was a nineteenth-century Democrat and had changed little since the time of Grover Cleveland. Truman appreciated the regularity of Garner's democracy, the invariable truth of his word, once given, just as he had appreciated that of Boss Tom. President Franklin D. Roosevelt deserted Garner in 1940 in favor of a new nominee for the vice-presidency, Secretary of Agriculture Henry A. Wallace, but Truman remained loyal to Garner.

Garner was one of the first men whom Truman came to like and admire during the ten years after 1935 when he was senator from Missouri. Among the others were Senator Burton K. (Burt) Wheeler of Montana, a maverick who seldom went along with the regular organization and always spoke his mind, but who was pleasant and kind. The great majority of senators ignored newcomer Truman, whom they considered the stooge of Boss Tom. A critic said that Truman had calluses on his ears from taking orders on the long-distance phone from Kansas City. Only a few senators, such men as Burt Wheeler and Carter Glass of Virginia, gave Truman any attention. Senator James F. Byrnes of South Carolina, who had been in the upper house since 1931, looked down his long nose at Truman and ignored him.

After some months, the president found time to see the new senator, and the meeting was cordial. Roosevelt took Truman for granted, however, for Truman voted an almost solid New Deal line. It was not that he was uncritical of legislation, that he had just run for office to earn a paycheck and keep off the streets. As presiding judge for a large metropolitan county and as the Missouri official in charge of federal relief for the state, he had seen what the federal government could do to relieve the needy. He had always believed that greedy businessmen had caused much of the squalor of the depression and that the needy deserved attention from government, immediately through relief and indirectly through laws to prevent their exploitation. Truman may have made a tactical mistake in voting regularly for New Deal measures, because he thereby made himself invisible to the president. The Missouri senator did not say much in the floor debates, for he felt he needed time to get acquainted with senate procedures and should not talk before he thought. Roosevelt gave most of the state's patronage to Clark, who took it as if it belonged to him. Thus, Truman's relations with Roosevelt during his first term were almost nonexistent.

Truman, who was not a man to forget slights but was unwilling to linger unduly or at least uselessly over them, went ahead with his work and believed he was in luck with his committee assignments: the Interstate Commerce Committee, the Appropriations Committee, and two minor committees—the Printing Committee, and the Public Buildings and Grounds Committee. Burt Wheeler, chairman of Interstate Commerce, got resolutions through authorizing his committee to organize the nation's airlines and draw up new rules for the railroads. A subcommittee that Truman chaired produced the Civil Aeronautics Act of 1938, which regulated the country's airlines for forty years. In addition, Truman could have had no better introduction to the economy of the United States than to sit on Wheeler's railroad subcommittee and help hammer out a major new enactment. The railroads needed investigation, for they were in deep trouble in the 1930s. The railroads' managers usually acted legally, but they watered stock by bringing out new issues without increasing assets, took huge salaries, and managed large expense accounts. They would sell their own real estate to companies at inflated prices or put relatives on the payroll. Through one device or another, they took money out of the railroads. Many of the roads were bankrupt, and the public was furious about the way in which good money had turned into bad stocks and bonds while the proprietors came out of reorganizations and changes of management wearing new suits of clothes. Wheeler's subcommittee planned to do something about it. At first, Truman simply asked to sit with the subcommittee; when his regular attendance and intense interest became obvious, Wheeler appointed him a member. Every night he took home a sheaf of papers and examined the ways in which high finance had operated against the public interest. The economic royalists, as he and President Roosevelt described the financiers, had laid their plans carefully and had siphoned off huge sums, loading the roads with debt that could not be serviced if the slightest reduction of income occurred. When the reckoning came in the 1930s, they stepped back from the mess they had created and watched railroad investments go down toward nothing, with the nation's economy going along. Their own incomes had been assured years earlier through purchase of real estate or other investments that would not suffer from the railroads' decline. Night after night Truman stayed up in the living room of his Washington apartment doing his homework, sighing to himself over the rascality of leaders of American railroad corporations and noticing that most of them were card-carrying members of the Republican party. At the end of his first term in the Senate, the Wheeler-Truman Bill became the Transportation Act of 1940.

During this period, the Truman family spent half its time in Washington in a succession of rented apartments and the other half in the house in Independence. For the senator's young daughter Margaret, a spindly ten-year-old when Truman first ran for the Senate and on the verge of becoming a young lady when that term was finished, the experience of moving in and out of the Independence public schools was not exhilarating, nor was the life in Washington in a cramped two-bedroom apartment, where she shared a room with Grandmother Wallace. Her parents constantly sought to save money from a $10,000 senatorial salary that hardly kept them afloat in their two residences, not to mention the cost of traveling and occasional entertaining. Senator Truman was unable to get out of debt, even though he took the expedient of putting Bess on the payroll; Bess, it should be said, came to the office and worked like everyone else. It was a narrow and uninteresting life for the daughter of a senator, enhanced occasionally by an expedition up or down Connecticut Avenue to buy an ice cream soda or to look at the expensive stores where wives and daughters of representatives and senators with private incomes made their purchases.

In 1940, Senator Truman's political life entered a crisis unlike any he had faced before. It was serious trouble, and no one offered to help him as Boss Tom had in 1934. It could not be repaired over a period of years, like the failure of the haberdashery, and he was to remember it for the rest of his life. Truman's problem in 1940 was the ambitious governor of Missouri, Lloyd Stark, proprietor of a famous nursery that produced the Stark apples known nation-wide. Stark had become the governor with the support of Boss Tom Pendergast. When the boss got into trouble over voting frauds in the general election in 1936 and his income tax returns proved to be out of order, the Roosevelt administration found him embarrassing.

Senator Bennett Clark took the opportunity for revenge against Boss Tom, and Stark turned on his benefactor and supported a federal district attorney who sent the boss to federal prison. Stark then began to show friendship to the Roosevelt administration, and it was reciprocated. He came to Washington for friendly chats with the president, and there was talk of a cabinet post. In his Washington trips Stark sometimes was too busy to stop by the offices of the junior senator from Missouri. In the spring of 1940, however, when Stark was visiting in the capital, he stopped in at Truman's outer office in the Senate Office Building and told Truman's secretary, Vic Messall, that he, the governor, would never think of running against the senator in the forth-coming Democratic primary. Truman knew instantly that Stark was going to run, and he did. Even Truman's closest supporters hesitated to fight Stark in the primary contest. He was backed by the Roosevelt administration, while Truman's mentor, Boss Tom, was in prison. Truman held a meeting in St. Louis to decide what to do. Half of those he asked to the meeting did not show up, and the other half saw only defeat facing the senator. Truman then said he would run even if he received only his own vote.

The contest moved back and forth, with no sure signs of the outcome, until Stark's egotism eventually began to shine forth. The governor had cut too large a swath in the state; among other things, he forced his police bodyguards to salute him and gave the impression that he owned the state. Truman's few friends resorted to the stratagem of getting Maurice Milligan, the victorious district attorney in Kansas City, into the race, and Milligan took some of the "good government" primary votes that otherwise might have gone to Governor Stark. Senator Truman went into 78 of the 114 Missouri counties, speaking constantly for his record and for President Roosevelt, who fortunately did not endorse Stark, although he did not endorse Truman either. Truman squeaked through the election with a plurality of 7,976 votes.

Truman never forgave Governor Stark; he liked to say afterward that he had sent Stark back to the nursery. Some years later, however, when the pundits again announced that there was no hope for Truman's election to the presidency in 1948—when the pollster Elmo Roper declared that science had chosen Governor Thomas E. Dewey to be the next president of the United States, when the radio commentator H. V. Kaltenborn spent half of election night denying that Truman could be elected—Truman, who had come back to Independence to vote, went to a hotel in Excelsior Springs, Missouri, and slept soundly through the night. He had been in a tight spot before.

Thus Truman was reelected senator in 1940, taking the oath in early 1941, and the two great Missouri dailies that had opposed his election, the Kansas City *Star* and the St. Louis *Post-Dispatch*, were busily eating crow. Truman again set to work and soon turned to a project that ultimately made him available for the vice-presidential nomination in 1944 and thereby the presidency. His Missouri constituents had been telling him about the waste of public money in construction projects at the U.S. Army's bustling encampment at Fort Leonard Wood, where draftees were sent to begin their training. The stories were horrendous. Under cost-plus contracts, contractors paid any prices, any wages, to get their projects done as shoddily as they pleased, while the military officers refused to intervene because they felt the country had not supported them since the end of World War I. Senator Truman paid attention to his constituents' mail, which convinced him that army officers were having a holiday at Fort Leonard Wood. He had disapproved of regular officers ever since the day in 1918 when the 35th Division, to which Truman's 129th Field Artillery was attached, came out of combat dirty and disheveled and was upbraided by a colonel for not giving proper attention to the dress code. Absurd martinets, was Captain Truman's appraisal. He always believed the country's future lay in the hands of National Guard officers; in 1941 he was himself a Guard colonel. Unconvinced by the army's explanation that the situation at Leonard Wood was all right, he asked his fellow senators to authorize a special committee to look into defense expenditures.

The result was the Special Committee to Investigate the National Defense Program, chaired by the junior senator from Missouri. Truman let the White House know that he, a Democrat, was not going to start another committee of the sort that had bedeviled Lincoln during the Civil War. He would confine the committee's work to factual investigations and to reports that would shame erring contractors and their business supporters into renegotiating contracts and arriving at decent and respectable charges. The White House was not impressed—although Senator Byrnes, who allowed the new committee's chairman the princely sum of $15,000 to investigate the expenditure of $25 billion, may not have been acting on instructions from the White House; it may have been but another sign that the veteran senator from South Carolina did not think much of the Missouri senator. Undaunted, Truman went ahead and enlisted a serious committee of six other senators to work at investigating the national defense program, and he used most of his initial appropriation to hire a first-rate lawyer, Hugh Fulton, to manage the investigation.

Truman barely had organized the investigating committee when war came with a suddenness that caught every American up short in surprise, astonishment, and disbelief that the impossible had happened. Talk of war had been everywhere, but no one thought it could happen, especially in the Pacific. When the news came on the radio that Sunday afternoon in December 1941 (all the regular programs were interrupted by announcers relating the Japanese attack on Hawaii and the Pacific fleet), it was incomprehensible. In the following days came the United States' declaration of war against Japan and the announcement by Germany and Italy that, in accord with their alliances with Japan, they too were at war with the United States.

Truman was a patriot from his Missouri roots, and he never doubted the rightness of the Allied cause, the evil machinations of enemy nations, and especially the malign purposes of Nazi Germany. He was sure from the outset that the United States would win, and he wanted to do his best for the cause. He tried to get into the army; in full uniform as a colonel in the National Guard, he marched into the office of the army's chief of staff, General George C. Marshall, and asked to go on active duty. The general looked up at the senator and without a trace of diplomacy, said, "We don't need any old stiffs like you." Truman argued with Marshall, pointing out that he was four years younger than the general, but there was nothing more he could do. Marshall advised the senator to go back to Congress, where he could do more good than he could as only a colonel in the army. Senator Truman watched proudly while Vivian's sons took part in the war. His cousin, Major General Ralph Truman, had stayed in the reserves between the wars and in 1940–1941 was commanding general of the 35th Division, the senator's old division in World War I, when it was called to federal service. Like almost all the reserve generals, Ralph was relieved of duty and spent the war on inactive status; Senator Truman realized that Ralph, like himself, was too old for service. Ralph's son, a graduate of West Point, rose to the rank of colonel, and his Uncle Harry was proud.

Realizing that the war had to be fought by younger men, Senator Truman concentrated on what he could do, which was to turn the investigating committee into the best organization he could, so as to help the United States win against its enemies. In this work he managed a triumph almost as gratifying as if he had been on the battlefield, and he was rightly proud of his work. The Truman Committee, as it became known, turned out to be a model senate committee. It looked at the seamy side of the war effort—in Truman's words, "contractors on camp construction, airplane engine manufacturers who made faulty ones, steel plate factories which cheated, and hundreds of other such sordid and unpatriotic ventures." The committee investigated procurement, labor hoarding, and army and navy waste of food and other supplies, but it concluded that, by and large, this war effort was the greatest production and war preparation job in history.

The committee, acting by unanimous vote and releasing its reports only after every member agreed, investigated rubber production, cartel agreements between the great oil and aluminum companies, and labor leaders who were willing to sacrifice the country for their own benefit. Malefactors hastened to retreat from their activities, however, when the committee focused on their wrongdoing. General Brehon B. Somervell, in charge of army supply, told President Roosevelt that the committee saved the country $15 billion.

In the summer of 1944, rumors of a Truman-for-vice-president boom began to be heard. The senator brushed them off; he was happy in the Senate, doing what he wanted, and he had no desire to be vice-president. But the rumors had more substance than he had imagined; in the early part of the summer a group of party regulars got together and talked President Roosevelt into accepting Truman as the vice-presidential nominee at the Chicago convention of the Democratic party in July.

The main reason for this surprising turn of events was that the party's chieftains, mostly big city bosses, vehemently opposed the reelection of Vice-President Henry Wallace, whom they considered a dreamer. He wrote and spoke well, but the old guard party members thought he represented the left wing of the New Deal. Wallace had never really run for office. He did not like to talk politics, preferring to deal with issues, and his influence in the Senate during his vice-presidency was nil. The party regulars therefore chose Truman, a man after their own hearts, who could be counted on when he gave his word. They felt he was well prepared for the White House if destiny were to place him there.

In this respect, the regulars had made a calculation that President Roosevelt refused to make. Roosevelt was desperately ill but refused to acknowledge the fact. The pallor of death was about him. That autumn, while making a speech in Bremerton, Washington, after a rigorous sea trip to the Pacific, where he had met the army and navy commanders in Hawaii, Roosevelt suffered an attack of angina pectoris. He barely got through the speech without his listeners, most of whom were hearing him on the radio, discerning any trouble. Roosevelt's blood pressure had been rising, and he had been careless about the signs, which may have been explained to him delicately. Many years later, Truman's counsel in the White House, Clark Clifford, said that, in his last months, Roosevelt thought that he would live forever. As he long had been accustomed to holding all the strings of national political influence, it was a formidable task to get him to change his mind about the vice-presidency, and the quickest way to political purgatory was to mention the chief's health.

In a White House meeting on July 11, however, the minor chieftains did obtain the president's consent to drop Vice-President Wallace in favor of either Truman or Justice William O. Douglas of the Supreme Court. Truman's name was mentioned first in a handwritten note that the chairman of the Democratic National Committee, Robert E. Hannegan of St. Louis, extracted from the president right after the White House meeting and in a later typed version obtained when Roosevelt's railway car stood in a siding at Chicago, en route to the West Coast.

In the selection of the vice-presidential candidate at Chicago that summer, matters became extremely delicate. There may well have been more than one presidential note circulating. According to the later testimony of Roosevelt's secretary, Grace Tully, who had typed the note mentioning Truman and Douglas, the handwritten note from which she had typed put Douglas's name before Truman's, and Hannegan maneuvered the change at Chicago. Hannegan died a few years later, however, and his papers were destroyed. In 1950, Truman sought to reconstruct what happened, and he was certain that Hannegan had not engaged in monkey business. He remembered a second note Hannegan showed him, written on a scratch pad from the president's desk, which said, "Bob, it's Truman. FDR." Truman tried to get this second note from Mrs. Hannegan, but she could not find it.

After Wallace, Senator Byrnes of South Carolina was the leading declared candidate for the vice-presidency at the convention. He had resigned to become an associate justice of the Supreme Court and had then left that post to serve as the president's principal assistant, a virtual "assistant president for the home front," who drew criticism that otherwise would have focused on Roosevelt. The president encouraged both Byrnes and Wallace to seek second place on his ticket. He wrote a letter to Wallace saying that, if he were a delegate to the convention, he would vote for Wallace. He did not have the decency to tell either candidate that he had switched to Truman. There was enormous activity at the Chicago convention, for both Byrnes and Wallace knew the presidency was at stake—everyone was sure that Roosevelt would be reelected and would probably die in office.

Wallace lost because, after giving him a letter of support, the president refused to give him anything more. He did his best to get the nomination anyway. Someone had counterfeited convention tickets, and Wallace not only packed his supporters into the galleries but got them onto the convention floor. The convention organist was playing, "Iowa, Iowa, that's where the tall corn grows"—the Wallace fight song. Then the old guard politicians in charge of the convention took over, however. One of them threatened to cut the organ's cable with a fire axe, and another announced a temporary recess.

The tactics used against Byrnes may have been more delicate and possibly were instigated by the president. The national chairman, Hannegan, told Byrnes that the president was for him, even after Hannegan had met with the president in his private railroad car and had received the note naming Truman. Hannegan also explained that Byrnes would surely be able to obtain the support of such labor leaders present at the convention as Philip Murray of the Congress of Industrial Organizations (CIO) and Sidney Hillman, president of the Amalgamated Clothing Workers Union. Murray agreed to support Byrnes, but Hillman would not bend "under any condition." During the war, Byrnes had obtained a reputation of being antilabor, because in his role as presidential advisor it had been necessary to control the demands of unions. It is possible that, during the war, President Roosevelt had anticipated Byrnes's candidacy for high office and had killed his chances by giving him that job. In any event, it is interesting that, when Hannegan reported Hillman's position to Roosevelt on July 19, the president already knew it, having met with Hillman on July 12. On July 14, knowing Hillman's point of view, the wily president advised Hannegan about Byrnes's nomination, saying, "Clear it with Sidney." In later recountings of Byrnes's defeat, it was said that he had been "Sidneyed."

The nomination finally went to the senator from Missouri, who almost to the end refused to believe that he was Roosevelt's nominee. Hannegan called him to a meeting at the Blackstone Hotel, where Truman found several of the convention leaders assembled. In his presence, Hannegan placed a call to Roosevelt, who by that time was on the West Coast. When the connection was made, Truman was sitting on one twin bed and Hannegan was across from him on the other. When the president used the phone he always talked in such a loud voice that it was necessary to hold the phone away from one's ear to keep from being deafened, so Truman could easily hear both ends of the conversation.

"Bob," Roosevelt said, "have you got that fellow lined up yet?"

"No," answered Hannegan, "he is the contrariest Missouri mule I've ever dealt with."

"Well, you tell him if he wants to break up the Democratic Party in the middle of a war, that's his responsibility," said the president, and hung up the phone with a bang.

Stunned, Truman sat for a minute or two and then began walking around the room. All the people in the room were watching him and not saying a word. At last he said, "Well, if that is the situation I'll have to say yes, but why the hell didn't he tell me in the first place."

At that point, in the summer of 1944, Truman had no opportunity to think at length and deeply about the situation in which he found himself, for a grand chapter in the life of the Republic was closing. Roosevelt was a man whom Americans of both parties had watched in the presidency with fascination, a man with an overwhelming presence. He had been in office nearly a dozen years, and Truman knew he would be reelected. The human quality of this handsome man impressed everyone who came in contact with him. People went into his office thinking they were going to tell Roosevelt something, and prepared themselves for argument, only to find themselves charmed and often unable even to state their cases. They left the president's presence with a feeling they were walking on air, certain in the knowledge that he had agreed with them, supported them, and looked to further association, although none of these things may have been the case. Roosevelt was as impressive publicly as he was in private, and his travels across the country by train and automobile were almost regal; everywhere people came out to see the handsome, smiling president. In addition, his was the finest oratorical voice of his generation, perhaps of the century. Early in his administration, President Roosevelt undertook what he described as fireside chats, informal talks to the American people by radio, and these conversational discussions of the state of the country dominated the air waves, mesmerizing listeners, at a time when everyone desired strong national leadership. The New Deal's measures were welcome, and many were successful, but the dominant factor in restoring national confidence in the 1930s was the president of the United States and his reassuring radio talks. It was possible to walk down any street of an American city on a summer evening when the president was on the radio and hear his voice coming from the open doors and windows of living rooms as one walked—for everyone listened to the president.

During the war, the president had also been dominant in foreign affairs, and the feeling everywhere, at home and abroad, was that he was supervising the highest policies of state, that control lay in his hands. The personality of the president assured everyone of American actions, American purposes. As readers looked at the newspaper photographs of Roosevelt and Churchill in conference, there never was a feeling that FDR was a subordinate figure in the presence of the majestic Churchill. The president radiated authority in foreign policy as well as in domestic affairs.

This, then, was the man with whom Truman was running. If the Missouri senator could have paused during the remaining weeks of the summer of 1944 or the autumn of that year, he would have shaken his head in disbelief to think not only that he, Harry S. Truman, was running with such a man but that sometime in the next months or years he might succeed Roosevelt in the White House. The president's health was rapidly declining, and Truman knew it. Out on the circuit that autumn, going from city to city lambasting the Republican candidate, Governor Thomas E. Dewey of New York, Truman knew he was running for the presidency, and he quietly told a few friends that the president was not apt to survive a fourth term. When Truman and Roosevelt lunched at a table on the White House lawn shortly after the Chicago convention, the president's hand shook so badly he could hardly pour cream into his coffee. Truman was appalled at his physical condition.

The issues during the campaign of 1944 were almost non-existent; it was a campaign of personalities. Both major parties backed United States participation in some form of postwar international organization to maintain world peace and security. Dewey's running mate was Senator John W. Bricker of Ohio. Neither Republican candidate aroused public enthusiasm, although the popular vote for Roosevelt and Truman was not a landslide—25,602,505 for the Democrats, 22,006,278 for the Republicans. In the electoral college the vote was more decisive, 432 to 99.

Having been elected with Roosevelt in November 1944, Truman took office at a ceremony held, contrary to custom, at the south side of the White House. He thereafter presided carefully and regularly over the Senate. He saw the president only a few times after the inauguration, usually in the company of other people. He was not privy to the great secrets of state, military or diplomatic—the Manhattan Project for manufacture of nuclear weapons or the secret agreements negotiated early in February 1945 at the Yalta Conference with Prime Minister Churchill of Great Britain and Premier Stalin of the Soviet Union.

Truman's time between January and April 1945 passed in a round of busyness not quite like his earlier Senate days, for he no longer had the press of constituents. There was much ceremony, especially official dinners and receptions, for the president was out of the city and the country a great deal and, even when available, did not get around as easily as the vice-president. The Trumans did what ceremony required but preferred the privacy of their Connecticut Avenue apartment for the little time they had together.

It was a strange interlude. Truman always had risen to challenges, but his first weeks as vice-president held none. In past years, the president's health had gone up and down, and the previous summer and autumn it had been down. When Roosevelt returned from Yalta he sat in the well of the House and uncharacteristically asked the joint session of Congress to excuse him from standing because of the ten pounds of steel he carried on his legs—the braces he wore as a result of polio. He looked pale and he stumbled through his speech, unable to speak clearly or pace his text. He then went down to Warm Springs, Georgia, for a rest.

It was one thing for Truman to know that Roosevelt's health was too shaky to last another four years and that the presidency of the United States lay ahead. It was something else to realize, as he did on April 12, 1945, that he, Harry S. Truman, had become president. Late that afternoon, after presiding over a tiresome session of the Senate, the vice-president walked through the main part of the Capitol to the House side, where he was to meet with a few congressional friends in the "board of education" room, a hideaway presided over by Speaker Sam Rayburn, to have a drink or two. When he arrived there, he learned that Steve Early, one of Roosevelt's aides, had called from the White House and asked that he return the call at once. He placed the call and Early, in a tight voice, asked him to come to the White House immediately. Before his friends could ask the obvious question, Truman put up his hand and, white faced, strode out the door. When his limousine arrived at the White House that darkening afternoon, he went into Mrs. Roosevelt's study to find her with her daughter, Anna Roosevelt Boettiger, her daughter's husband, and Early. Mrs. Roosevelt placed her arm gently around his shoulder and said, "Harry, the president is dead." Truman asked what he could do for her, and the response, so typical of that great lady, was, "Is there anything *we* can do for *you*? For you are the one in trouble now."

There followed a hurried summons to the cabinet and other high officials and the swearing-in ceremony, held at the end of the cabinet table. A photograph of the ceremony shows officials crowded into the picture on both sides, and a portrait of Woodrow Wilson looking down from the wall, behind Truman's serious face and uplifted hand, his other hand clasping the Bible. The time on the clock under the portrait was 7:09.

The new president went by limousine back to the little apartment on Connecticut Avenue. A neighbor woman made him a ham sandwich, as he had had no dinner, and then he went to bed and slept soundly, as was his custom on all occasions, high or low. The following morning he returned to the White House, where an aide who peeked into the Oval Office beheld him sitting behind the enormous presidential desk, swiveling idly back and forth, regarding the pictures on the wall around the impressive room. Truman was looking about uncertainly, his eyes peering from behind his thick-lensed glasses. At that moment he appeared as uncertain as Americans in general were about what he would do in the presidency.

Knowing that his predecessor had lost touch with Congress, especially the Senate, where his own roots were, Truman decided to pay a visit to the upper house and have lunch with his friends. That lunch gave him his first feeling of what it meant to be president. Roosevelt's successor drove up to the Hill and shook hands boisterously, showing no evidence of his new dignity, with the men he had known for so long from meetings in the cloakroom and dining room as well as on the floor. The lunch seemed to be successful. Afterward, he shook hands again with everyone in sight, including his young friends, the pages. Eventually, the handshaking over, the new president drove back down the avenue toward the White House. But he had felt a certain uneasiness in the behavior of his former colleagues, who were beginning to draw the lines of dignity between themselves and the man in whom all the power of the executive branch of the government now rested. It was the end, he sensed, of the old familiar ties.

This is the place I told Stalin about the Atom Bomb, which was exploded July 16, 1945 in New Mexico. He did not realize what I was talking about!

HST

Potsdam

III

Year of Decisions

WOODROW WILSON told a Princeton friend in 1913 that it would be the irony of fate if his administration had to deal with foreign affairs; he expected to deal with domestic legislation. In view of Harry S. Truman's training in domestic politics, his elevation to the presidency was similarly ironic. He dealt with domestic policies in 1945 and thereafter, of course, but he spent much more time on foreign affairs. At the beginning of his presidency, the war was in its final stages in Europe and the Far East, and every change in the military scene brought problems. He knew nothing about these problems and had to start at the beginning, as he had in Jackson County politics twenty-two years before. Here the parallel with the Wilson administration ends; the president of 1913–1921 had several years to learn, but Truman had to act at once.

In the first volume of his memoirs, *Year of Decisions*, Truman described his first year in the White House as a dramatic confrontation between a Missouri president and the international problems he inherited. Some concerns of the time later appeared to be less important than Truman had believed, and perhaps he was not very decisive; but 1945 was an initial year well worth looking back to, to see what went right with making peace in Europe and the Far East and what went wrong in relations with Soviet Russia.

That year marked the decline of wartime comradeship among the Allies and the emergence of the Soviet-American rivalry known as the Cold War. At the time Truman took office, relations with the Soviet Union had not been going well, and the president found he had inherited an awkward situation. The trouble went back to the tactics and strategy of the recent war. The sheer distance between the Eastern and Western fronts had made it difficult to coordinate strategy, and each part of the Allied coalition against the Germans tended to fight its own war.

Russia had been devastated by the German invasion of 1941 and the subsequent occupation of large parts of the USSR, which lasted until 1944. Nonetheless, on the Eastern front, the Soviets had taken on and eventually defeated the great majority of German divisions, making it much easier for the Western allies to attack through France and enter Germany by the end of the war. The German attack and occupation gravely injured Russia; losses in soldiers, civilians, and property were enormous.

These inequities grated on the Russians, but the most telling source of their resentment, the single fact that they never forgot in dealing with Western leaders, was the long delay in opening the second, Western front—the front that would take pressure off the Soviets fighting in the east. To no avail, Churchill and Roosevelt told Stalin, and their commanders told any Soviet general who would listen, that it was impossible to attack in France in 1942 and in 1943; only in 1944 were the American troops, who were essential to the task, ready in numbers and equipment. To the Soviets, however, the protests disguised Western willingness to follow the tactics occasionally suggested by some people in Britain and the United States, including then-senator Truman. When the Germans attacked the Russians in June 1941, Truman said that it was a marvelous opportunity to let the two totalitarian regimes fight each other to a standstill, and that when either was in danger of losing, the United States should give it enough help to resume the attack. Truman made this remark in singular ignorance, but it was reminiscent of a not-uncommon attitude in England in the late 1930s—that a strong Nazi Germany might have the virtue of containing communism. The Soviets believed that the Western allies waited until the last moment, when it was clear that the USSR was going to survive, and then went into France so as to enter Germany by the back door and get everything possible out of a German surrender.

The wartime conferences of the Big Three—Roosevelt, Churchill, and Stalin—had been uneasy exercises, in which the Western allies sought to show good faith and Stalin attempted to take pledges of military assistance. The meeting at Teheran in November–December 1943 was largely for getting acquainted. The Yalta Conference of early February 1945 seemed a fateful affair by the time Truman became president, for it appeared that Roosevelt's physical weakness might have produced mental lethargy. It was clear that the Yalta Conference was not a Western victory. This meeting at the resort in the Crimea had taken place just after the Western allies had beaten back the Germans in the Battle of the Bulge and were uncertain of their military position, having been rocked by Hitler's surprise marshaling of divisions in the Ardennes forest. Moreover, at Yalta the Western allies spent most of their time arguing over the postwar government and boundaries of Poland, an embarrassing subject because the protection of Poland, guaranteed futilely by Britain and France in 1939, had been the immediate cause of the war. The Russian army occupied almost all of Poland by the time of the Yalta Conference, and there was little the Westerners could do to protect the Poles, other than obtain Russian signature of the Yalta Declaration on Liberated Europe, a list of civil rights and liberties promised to the peoples of the occupied countries. At Yalta the United States also sought and obtained a Soviet promise to enter the Far Eastern war within three months of the end of hostilities in Europe, another testimony to Western weakness. At that time, the Japanese were fighting fanatically at Okinawa, the nuclear bomb had not been tested, and the U.S. Army anticipated that the war in the Pacific could last into 1946.

In the early months of 1945, the approach of victory, which even the Westerners sensed, despite the Battle of the Bulge, made the Soviets ever more difficult, for they saw less reason to compromise with the West. This was the situation when the

American prisoners in Germany were liberated by advancing troops of the USSR; the Soviets did not seem concerned about the liberated prisoners and left them to fend for themselves, getting back to American lines as best they could. The United States government took offense at this callousness, perhaps not realizing that, to the Soviets, prisoners were useless human material, to toss aside in favor of more important concerns of an ongoing war. The Soviet Union also had no interest in its own prisoners in Germany, blaming them for surrendering rather than fighting to the finish.

There were other irritations, as well, such as Soviet behavior when German envoys met American officers in Switzerland to negotiate a surrender in Italy. Stalin accused the Americans of taking surrenders without telling the Soviet Union. Behind the sharpness of Stalin's cables, which infuriated Roosevelt, was his suspicion that German troops would hold their lines against Russian armies in Eastern Europe and cooperate with the Western allies in a last-minute coalition between capitalist countries against the proletarian Eastern ally that had held the Germans in 1941–1944.

Such clashes may have made the Soviets prickly about the prerogatives in regard to American lend-lease aid—aid that the president could award any nation deemed worthy of support, in accord with an act of Congress in March 1941. The Soviet Union never had negotiated lend-lease, as the other allied nations had, but took whatever it could get and always asked for more. Lend-lease protocols with other nations were stiff agreements, sometimes involving a quid pro quo—in the case of Britain, the feeding of American troops stationed in England in exchange for lend-lease aid. In the spring of 1945, the Soviets asked for all sorts of deliveries, such as entire rubber and steel plants, items of little use in the war against Germany and quite probably in the war against Japan. Lend-lease negotiators were uneasy about the $11 billion the Soviets received, more than a fifth of all American lend-lease. They feared that postwar Congresses might raise a point of constitutionality because of the loose protocols and might question the right of the administrators to give away so much. A few days after the German surrender on May 8, 1945, Truman's lend-lease administrator ended all lend-lease to the USSR, turning ships around in mid-ocean, in accord with an order that Truman signed with insufficient thought. Premier Stalin sent a sharp cable, and President Truman resumed deliveries.

Against this backdrop of increasing Soviet-American distrust, Harry S. Truman succeeded Roosevelt in the presidency in April 1945. His first decision was whether to go ahead with the planned conference in San Francisco where the United Nations charter would be drawn up. With little deliberation, the new president said that everything would continue as it had, that the conference would meet and, he hoped, would prove successful. The United Nations seemed a worthwhile organization to the new president, who had regretted the failure of Wilson's League of Nations. In the United Nations as established in San Francisco, the great powers dominated the upper house, known as the Security Council. A veto by a permanent member of the council, one of the great powers, ended any chance of decision there. The lower house, known as the General Assembly, was for debate, not decision. (In 1950 the United States went to the General Assembly for a decision—a vote of confidence about extending the Korean War into North Korea—thus creating a precedent. At the time, the United States did not sense how difficult it would be to control the Assembly in the future, because of the rapidly increasing numbers of new nations; the family of nations expanded from sixty at the beginning of World War II to three times that in the 1980s.)

Shortly before the lend-lease disagreement, Truman learned that the Soviet Union's foreign minister, Vyacheslav Molotov, was not planning to attend the San Francisco conference. This greatly displeased the president, who believed that the Soviets were showing no interest in the new world organization. Molotov did attend the conference.

Molotov stopped in Washington en route to San Francisco,

and his meeting with Truman there was much commented on after the war as marking a downturn in relations. What happened was not so much a downturn as a punctuation mark in the gradually lessening wartime cooperation between the superpowers (the new word that began to be heard that year). Molotov went to the White House to pay his respects, and the president let the Soviet foreign minister know that he considered Soviet behavior in Poland to be contrary to the Yalta agreements; he described Soviet behavior as a one-way street. In their conversation, Truman was not very diplomatic; according to the State Department's interpreter, Charles E. Bohlen, the president employed swear words. "I've never been talked to like that in my life," Molotov said. "Carry out your agreements," snapped the president, "and you won't get talked to like that." The conversation had been rehearsed, of course. Truman had previously discussed the Russian situation with his advisers, including Ambassador W. Averell Harriman, who had flown in from Moscow to bolster the president's opposition to the Russians.

Although this was a period of uncertainty and distrust between the USSR and the Western allies, Truman's conversation with Molotov could not be considered the beginning of what came to be known as the Cold War. Six weeks after that meeting, the president was still cooperating with the Russians, issuing an order that brought American troops in Germany back more than a hundred miles into the zone allotted them at Yalta. These troops had gone into the Soviet area in the final days of the war, and Churchill had beseeched Truman to keep them there as a guarantee of Russian good behavior. After consulting with General Eisenhower, however, who agreed that it was necessary for the United States to cooperate with the Russians, Truman ordered the troops back.

Meanwhile, the war in Europe ended on Truman's sixty-first birthday. The Soviets fought their way into Germany from the east and the Western allies came in from the south and west. American and Soviet troops met at Torgau, fifty miles south of Berlin along the Elbe, on April 27. A few days later, Hitler committed suicide in his command bunker in Berlin. The Germans surrendered to the allies on both fronts on May 8.

For the Americans, war's end did not lead to an immediate conference with the Russians, although Churchill called for one. Truman wanted to wait until the San Francisco conference had drawn up the United Nations charter. He also may have wanted to delay long enough to test the atomic bomb at Alamogordo, New Mexico, where the army was preparing to suspend and detonate a test device from a steel tower in the midst of the desert sands. The Potsdam Conference finally began in mid-July. President Truman and his advisers had just reached Potsdam when news arrived of a successful bomb test on July 16, 1945. Insiders at the meeting who knew about the nuclear weapon noticed Truman's enthusiastic reception of the news, and some thought that his perky behavior at the conference derived from his feeling that he and his country now possessed a wonderful, perhaps diabolical, ace in the hole—that the American bargaining position at Potsdam had improved dramatically.

Whether Truman took advantage of his new knowledge remains a moot question. The president's recently discovered diary of the Potsdam Conference—written on scrap paper and lost until it turned up in the Truman Library in 1979—gives no indication that he felt in a particularly strong bargaining position. He did think the Japanese would fold up before the Russians came in, but he saw no way to use this result to ensure better Russian behavior. He found it difficult to be lighthearted after touring the wrecked city of Berlin, where the smell of death was everywhere and the scenes of devastation appalled him. He beheld bedraggled German civilians on the roads, pushing their belongings in carts and baby carriages, abject symbols of military defeat.

At the conference, the quiet good temper of his Russian counterpart, Stalin, at first charmed him; he found Stalin much more impressive than Churchill, who tried to flatter him. Truman wrote about his meeting with the ruler of Russia on July 17: "Promptly a few minutes before twelve I looked up from the desk and there stood Stalin in the doorway." The president got up and advanced to meet him, and Stalin held out his hand and smiled. "After the usual polite remarks we got down to business. I told Stalin that I am no diplomat but usually said yes & no to questions after hearing all the argument." Most of the big points, Truman noted, were settled. "He'll be in the Jap War on August 15th. Fini Japs when that comes about." The two leaders had lunch, talked amiably, and according to Truman, "put on a real show drinking toasts to everyone, then had pictures made in the back yard. I can deal with Stalin. He is honest—but smart as hell."   .

The president had met Churchill for the first time the previous day. Truman had arranged for the prime minister to call at 11:00 A.M. Churchill was there on the dot, but his daughter Diana noted that he had not been up so early in ten years, whereas the president had been up for four and a half hours. They had a pleasant conversation, and the president wrote that his British opposite was "a most charming and a very clever person—meaning clever in the English not the Kentucky sense. He gave me a lot of hooey about how great my country is and how he loved Roosevelt and how he intended to love me etc. etc. Well. I gave him as cordial a reception as I could—being naturally (I hope) a polite and agreeable person. I am sure we can get along if he doesn't try to give me too much soft soap. You know soft soap is made of ash hopper lye and it burns to beat hell when it gets into the eyes. It's fine for chigger bites but not so good for rose complexions. But I haven't a rose complexion."

On July 18 the president, who had been chosen chairman of the group, presented three proposals from the Big Three foreign ministers—procedures for peace negotiations and territorial settlements, political authority of the allied control council for Germany, and execution of the Yalta agreement on Poland— and "banged them through in short order, much to the surprise of Mr. Churchill. Stalin was very much pleased. Churchill was too, after he had recovered." That day the president wrote in his diary that he was not going to stay around "this terrible place" all summer just to listen to speeches, that "I'll go home to the Senate for that."

But when Churchill left the conference in mid-course, returning to London to learn the results of the parliamentary election held weeks before but delayed in order to count soldier votes, Truman was becoming fond of him and was aware of how the war had weakened the British empire. Moreover, Churchill's successor at the conference table after the Conservatives lost the election, the Labor party leader Clement Attlee, proved a weak substitute for the greatest statesman in British history. By the end of the conference, Truman also was irritated by Russian incivility. In the closing hours of the conference he had sought to interest the Soviets in a proposal to open the major waterways and canals of the world, and Stalin disdainfully refused even to include a reference to the proposition in the conference protocol.

As the meetings sagged, so did Truman's spirits. On July 24, after one of the sessions, the president carefully walked around the table to Stalin and told the Soviet leader the United States had tested a bomb of great explosive power. It was a touchy conversation, planned with advice from Churchill. In a joint Anglo-American effort—the British had been involved in the nuclear weapons project from the beginning—a device had been tested successfully; the British and the Americans felt they needed to say something to their Soviet ally. Truman did not tell Stalin that the test had involved a nuclear device. Without much visible emotion, Stalin said he hoped the Americans would use the new weapon on the Japanese, and he walked away. What Truman did not realize was that, when the premier got out of earshot, he discussed the matter with Molotov and Marshal Gregory Zhukov and decided to resume the Soviet atomic bomb project, which had languished during the war. Russian spies had penetrated the Manhattan Project at its highest levels, but Truman did not suspect this until the following September, when a Soviet code clerk defected from the Russian embassy in Ottawa. Sensing the downward drift of the conference, however, the president began to reflect on the nature of Russian communism, which, he noted, was "just police government pure and simple. A few top hands just take clubs, pistols, and concentration camps and rule the people on the lower levels." Nazis and fascists were worse, he felt, but "the rest are a bad lot, from the standpoint of the people who do not believe in tyranny." On July 30 he sadly recorded that Russia and Poland had agreed on the Oder and Western Neisse rivers as their border, "a unilateral arrangement without so much as a by your leave." The president spoke of his offer to open the waterways of the world, and what it would mean for Central Europe: "Our only hope for good from the European War is restored prosperity to Europe and future trade with them. It is a sick situation at best." Truman left Berlin on August 2, glad to get away from "that awful city."

On August 6, on his way home aboard the heavy cruiser *Augusta*, he was informed that the first nuclear bomb had been dropped on a Japanese city, Hiroshima. Exhilarated, he announced it to the officers in the ship's mess and to members of the crew. He had a feeling that the war in the Far East would end shortly, perhaps before the Russians entered. The ship docked at Newport News, Virginia, on August 9, the day of the second explosion, above Nagasaki, and the president returned to Washington in time to receive word the next day that the Japanese desired an armistice, which he granted August 14. The ceremony of surrender took place aboard the battleship *Missouri* in Tokyo Bay on September 2. Meanwhile, the Soviets had entered the war on August 8, between the two nuclear explosions. To get in before the war ended, they had come in a week ahead of Truman's expectations based on their Potsdam pledge. Had they waited until the middle of August, they would have missed the war by one day.

The war thus ended with the explosion of two nuclear bombs. This bothered Truman, who looked on nuclear weapons as almost beyond the bounds of civilized warfare. "We have discovered the most terrible bomb in the history of the world," his Potsdam diary notes. "The explosion was visible for more than 200 miles and audible for 40 miles and more. This weapon is to be used against Japan . . . so that military objectives and soldiers and sailors are the target and not women and children. Even if the Japs are savages, ruthless, merciless and fanatic, we as the leader of the world for the common welfare cannot drop this terrible bomb on the old capital [Kyoto] or the new [Tokyo]." When the bombs fell on Hiroshima and Nagasaki, however, they fell on every human being within the radius of destruction. This man with a Baptist conscience had permitted a decision that killed more than a hundred thousand Japanese, men, women, and children, condemned thousands more to frightful maiming, and shortened the life of everyone within the area of radiation.

In retrospect, it is clear that he made the decision to drop the bombs with insufficient forethought. The Manhattan Project had attained a momentum of its own, and everyone who knew about it assumed that, if the army was successful, the bombs would fall on Germany or Japan or both. Scientists were unsure about just what they were creating. They overestimated the TNT equivalent of the uranium (Hiroshima) bomb at 15,000 tons rather than 12,000, and they grossly underestimated the TNT equivalent of the plutonium (Nagasaki) bomb at between 500 and 1,000 tons when it amounted to 20,000. By the time the plutonium test was ready, the highest officials of the government, including the president, were at Potsdam, about to begin a difficult negotiation. Perhaps Truman should have warned the Japanese; the Potsdam Declaration by the United States and Britain, joined by Nationalist China—stating that Japan must surrender or face absolute and utter destruction—was not sufficiently specific. The army could have arranged a demonstration, perhaps exploding a weapon over Tokyo Bay in the early evening, with a blinding flash that would turn evening into daylight. Or so some scientists have suggested in retrospect. As it happened, two bombs were dropped within three days, hardly time enough to think what to do. Perhaps the second was superfluous. In any event the Japanese offered to surrender on August 10.

An often forgotten factor that strongly influenced Truman's

decision to drop the bombs was the behavior of the Japanese throughout the war. The beginning of the great conflict had been a surprise attack in which 2,400 Americans died; half of them drowned in the capsized hull of the battleship *Arizona*. Trapped sailors lived two or three weeks in the hull, breathing pockets of air in the upturned compartments. A few were fortunate enough to be close to the skin of the ship, and sailors in small boats alongside heard their tappings and were able to rip open the hull and free their shipmates. It was a horrible scene. In the Philippines after the fall of Bataan, prisoners were forced to march several dozen miles; 54,000 Filipinos and Americans reached Camp O'Donnell, but between 7,000 and 10,000 prisoners, of whom 2,300 were Americans, died en route from malaria, starvation, beatings, or execution. Throughout the war, the stories of Japanese mistreatment of prisoners were legion, and there were photographs showing barbaric behavior. In addition, reports of Japanese who jumped off cliffs or committed hara-kiri rather than surrender, or made mass banzai attacks, or suicidally crashed planes into ships lent credence to the belief that the Japanese were fanatics.

In later years, the president was sensitive about the bombings—his most criticized act. Publicly, he took the position that he had had no other possible course, and that the decision was easy, even knowing the momentous consequences for the people of Hiroshima and Nagasaki. In 1959 he told students at Columbia University that, after he ordered the bombs, he went to bed and slept soundly. He became irritated if anyone asked him why he dropped two nuclear bombs on the Japanese. The Truman Library contains countless letters to correspondents asserting that the buck stopped in his office, that he made the decision to drop the bombs and did not regret it because it saved not merely 250,000 or half a million American lives—soldiers and sailors and airmen who would have died in the invasion of Japan—but an equal number of Japanese lives that would have been lost. He believed he had made the best decision he could, given the information he had, and that no public man can be "constantly worrying about what history and future generations will say about decisions he has to make. He must live in the present, do what he thinks is right at the time, and history will take care of itself."

Privately, he was not so sure. The war was over and he could not change what had happened, but he had rethought his action. In cabinet meetings he stated that he wanted no more such weapons dropped on women and children. In 1945 the director of the budget said to him, "Mr. President, you have an atomic bomb up your sleeve." Truman replied, "Yes, but I am not sure it can ever be used." After the war, the army repeatedly sought custody of nuclear weapons, but the president resisted the efforts, maintaining that use of such weapons required a presidential decision. In retirement, Truman recalled the proposals of General MacArthur in 1950–1951 to widen the Korean War and shook his head in wonderment: "I could not bring myself to order the slaughter of 25 million noncombatants. . . . I just could not make the order for a Third World War."

After the war Truman sought an agreement with the Soviet Union regarding nuclear weapons. By that time it was evident that the Russians had infiltrated the Manhattan Project and knew the complicated technology necessary to obtain bomb materials and design both uranium and plutonium bombs. A committee chaired by Undersecretary of State Dean Acheson and assisted by a board of consultants chaired by David E. Lilienthal, head of the Tennessee Valley Authority, readied an American position on nuclear weapons: (1) the United States would retain its nuclear monopoly while the United Nations established an Atomic Development Authority to control all the world's dangerous fissionable materials and production plants; (2) there would be rigid on-the-spot inspections; and (3) any attempt by a nation to build nuclear weapons would become known to the Authority, which would report it to the nations of the world for appropriate sanctions. The organizer of American war production during World War I, Bernard M. Baruch, a conservative Democrat, presented the plan to the General Assembly and added his own injunction: no member of the Security Council would use the veto if a nation broke the nuclear agreement. This denial of the veto was an unnecessary issue, however, for only two nations—the United States and the USSR—could possibly have challenged the Atomic Development Authority. Because the plan provided for on-site inspection, the Soviet Union could not have continued its nuclear program, which had gone into high gear after Potsdam. The plan thus would have ensured Russian nuclear disarmament. Moreover, on-site inspection might have revealed the vulnerability of the USSR to the United States strategic air force at a time when the Soviets possessed no large bomber force.

The plan was not entirely against the Soviets, however; it did promise them virtual control of Europe, short of a major American or European rearmament. If the Russians had accepted the plan and the Americans had carried it out, the Soviets would have succeeded in removing the nuclear striking power of the United States while still maintaining a strong army with conventional weapons in Europe.

Sufficient reasons moved the Soviets to refuse the Baruch plan, but they had to couch refusal in careful terms, not just saying no. By the summer of 1947, they were stalling for time—asking for and indeed insisting on strict international control. No one knew what that meant. By 1948, the issue was deadlocked, and the Russians exploded their own nuclear test device on August 31, 1949.

At the conclusion of World War II, then, the international situation was disturbingly unsettled: formerly strong nations such as Britain and Germany had been weakened or shattered by the war; Soviet Russia and the United States seemed to be emerging as two hostile superpowers; and the technological advantage of the atomic bomb had altered the whole process of diplomacy and balance of power, as well as threatening a new and perhaps final holocaust. As his Year of Decision came to an end, residual problems from the war still occupied Truman. A

European peace conference at Paris, attended by the Big Four foreign ministers (United States, USSR, Britain, and France), drew up peace treaties for the defeated former Nazi satellites—Finland, Italy, Hungary, Bulgaria, and Rumania. Secretary of State James F. Byrnes spent months in Paris and, at the end of the year, signed treaties offering the former satellites a democratic future, with governments chosen by democratic means. The treaties resolved nothing, however, because the Red Army occupied most of these countries and dictated their politics. In several meetings during the first year of peace, the Big Four foreign ministers made rules for occupation of Germany and Japan, but, in the case of Germany, the Soviets and, to a lesser extent, the French refused to cooperate in supplying foodstuffs and protecting the currency. In Japan the Americans avoided interference with the occupation under General Douglas MacArthur by allowing the Soviet Union an advisory role; the Soviets were members of an advisory commission, but MacArthur had the right to issue interim directives.

Postwar tensions increased in early 1946 when a crisis arose with Russia over Iran. This large country on the border of the USSR had been an area of concern for the Russians since the nineteenth century. Historically, Iranian governments had been unresponsive to the needs of the Iranian people. Internal politics were dominated by large landowners and courtiers of the Shah's palace in Teheran, and foreign relations were controlled by the rivalries of Russia and Britain—with Britain especially concerned about the possible penetration of Russian influence into nearby India. In the twentieth century, exploitation of Iran's huge oil deposits added to the national and international confusions in Iran, creating riches for the Anglo-Iranian Oil Company and subsidies for its Iranian "retainers." The company arranged oil contracts to sell oil to the British navy at bargain prices, and it paid little for oil that went elsewhere. During World War II the British and the Russians had occupied Iran to ensure the transport of lend-lease supplies to Russia. In

1946, a crisis arose when the Soviets continued to maintain troops in the northern part of the country, contrary to a wartime agreement that set a date for their postwar departure.

The Soviets encouraged an Azerbaijani independence movement and prepared to divide the country as they had divided Germany, Austria, and Korea. Incensed, Truman undertook to pry the Russians out, nominally through the United Nations, where he counseled the Iranians to go for support.

Behind the impassioned pleas in the Security Council and General Assembly was Truman's demand that the Russians live up to their agreements. Some years later, in 1952, the president told a press conference that he had sent an ultimatum to the Russians in 1946 and they had removed their troops. He repeated this commentary in his memoirs, in his 1959 lectures at Columbia, and in conversation with the historian Herbert Druks in 1962. No record of such an ultimatum has appeared in the State Department files, but whether or not Truman sent an ultimatum, the Soviets did leave Iran in early 1946.

At about this time, signs of Soviet ill will toward the United States hardened into certainty. In 1946 the newspaperman Herbert B. Swope used the phrase "cold war," and Bernard Baruch employed it in a speech early the next year. Walter Lippmann picked it up for the title of a book. The phrase went back to German politics of the 1890s, and perhaps before that, and was singularly inappropriate in describing what happened after World War II because no war, of whatever sort, can be cold. But it described the neither-war-nor-peace atmosphere of the time, and people afterward talked of a Cold War.

In an effort to break through this situation, former Prime Minister Churchill accepted an offer of an honorary degree from Westminster College in Fulton, Missouri, the alma mater of Truman's military aide, Major General Harry H. Vaughan. Truman and Churchill traveled to Fulton by train from Washington, and during the trip the former British statesman showed the president his proposed remarks, which Truman declared admirable. On March 5, 1946, the two men marched down the aisle in the college gymnasium to the strains of "Love Divine, All Loves Excelling," a hymn that was well known to Truman but probably not listened to by Churchill, who hated all music except military marches. From the podium, Churchill delivered the famous "iron curtain" speech, in which he said that Russian actions in Europe had lowered an iron curtain between East and West. The speech created an uproar in the Kremlin, with Stalin comparing Churchill to Hitler. It also raised up a storm in the United States. Truman hedged about whether he had known what Churchill was going to say, but the former prime minister had issued a declaration, and the president sponsored it. The Year of Decisions thus came to an end indecisively, with announcements of Stalin's and Churchill's positions but not of Truman's.

One could properly ask whether Truman's experience or lack of it was good for the country—whether it was helpful to have a president who was ignorant of foreign affairs at the end of the greatest war in history and the beginning of the most awkward peace. To be sure, it was impossible to know what another president might have done, or even what Roosevelt would have done, when confronted with Russian intransigence. In his fourth inaugural address in January 1945 and again after the trip to Yalta, FDR showed clearly the need for sensitive diplomacy and especially the need to accept the reality of Soviet concerns for security, but FDR was disillusioned about the Russians shortly before his death. According to the testimony of one visitor, Anna Rosenberg, who lunched at the White House just before Roosevelt left for Warm Springs, after luncheon Roosevelt was handed a cable—Stalin's complaint about American handling of German surrenders in Italy—and "read it and became quite angry. He banged his fists on the arms of his wheelchair and said, 'Averell is right; we can't do business with Stalin. He has broken every one of the promises he made at Yalta.' " It is impossible to know whether Roosevelt would have told Molotov off about Poland, would have directed American troops to move back from the Russian zone in June 1945, would have tried to be

friendly and agreeable at Potsdam, would have ordered the
dropping of two nuclear bombs with no more questions than
Truman asked, would have sponsored the United Nations in the
form it took, would have stood up to the Russians over Iran, or
would have allowed Churchill to speak out as he did in this
country.

At first, the new president tried to do what his predecessor
might have done, in the knowledge that his countrymen had
elected him to the vice-presidency. As he felt more at home in
the office, he showed his natural independence, but he usually
acted only after consultation with advisers. It would have been
awkward to show independence in the company of the former
British prime minister, however, and Churchill took advantage
of Truman at Fulton; the president should never have looked at
the speech or commented on its excellence unless he was
prepared for the consequences.

Truman's uncertainties in 1945–1946 were in accord with
popular feeling. Americans did not favor stronger measures
than he advocated. Had his prescience been greater, had he
spoken with the tongues of angels, he could have accomplished
little more. A year after the hostilities in Europe and Asia, the
American people did not desire another war; they had had
enough. The American death toll in World War II had not been
as high as that of other nations—405,399 men dead, compared
to 6.1 million Russians, 3.2 million Germans, 1.2 million
Japanese, not to mention 6 million Jews, other people killed by
the Nazis, and air raid or other civilian deaths. Unlike in other
nations, there had been no physical destruction in America, no
bombing, and for years thereafter the United States was by far
the most powerful country in the world. But the exertion of the
conflict, and confusion about its end, raised questions for
Americans. At issue was the future of their foreign policy. Would
it be necessary to take part in the affairs of Europe and Asia for
the rest of the twentieth century? Would there be incessant

involvement, after a century and a half of certainty that there was a New World and an Old World and that two oceans protected American shores from foreign foes? The next year, 1947, brought the answers to these questions.

With Secretary Marshall

IV

Changing American
Foreign Relations

DURING Truman's presidency, three developments
dramatically changed American foreign policy: his announcement of the Truman Doctrine on March 12, 1947; the initial
appropriation for the Marshall Plan which passed Congress in
March 1948; and the North Atlantic Treaty of April 4, 1949, by
which the United States allied itself with foreign nations for the
first time since abrogation of the French Alliance in 1800.
President George Washington had established the tradition that
the country should remain apart from the ordinary combina-
tions and collisions of Europe. President Thomas Jefferson
announced a few years later that there should be no entangling
alliances. For a century and a half, American presidents followed
this policy of a New World and an Old World, of pretending to
be China to Europe's barbarians. Americans liked to maintain a
distance from Europe, and often celebrated its stupidities, but
all this ended during the Truman administration.

Truman's presence in the White House may not have been
essential to a change in the ancient policy, but without his
decisiveness there might have been a gradual and imperceptible
slide of American foreign relations toward an abyss that might
have widened into a third world war when the Soviets detonated
their nuclear test device in 1949 and began to manufacture
weapons in quantity.

Truman's achievements in foreign affairs rested on his appointment of first-class men to the Department of State—James F. Byrnes in the summer of 1945, George Marshall in January 1947, and Dean Acheson in January 1949. He then let them run their cabinet department with an eye to posterity rather than politics. The president still paid attention to the State Department. He disliked foreign service officers, whom he considered checked-suit wearers, white-spats boys, tea drinkers, and cookie pushers. Senator Alben Barkley told him about an American chargé d'affaires the senator had met in Cairo, who carried a cane and spoke like an Oxford graduate. Barkley had asked the man where he was from and had discovered that he came from Topeka, Kansas. Hearing the story, the president opined that this dandy, with his cane and checked suit, would have lasted about ten minues in the Kansas Hotel lobby in Topeka. Truman believed, however, that Byrnes and especially Marshall and Acheson were getting the checked-suit set in order, and when their recommendations came up for approval, he tended to do what they recommended.

Four men actually served as secretary of state under Truman, but Roosevelt had appointed the first, Edward R. Stettinius, Jr., who was considered inept. The late president had chosen Stettinius to succeed Cordell Hull in November 1944 because FDR wanted to run foreign affairs himself. Stettinius was a handsome figurehead, with a ready smile, prematurely white hair, and bushy black eyebrows that asserted the youthfulness denied by the white hair—and he never knew what went on in the State Department. A story had it that he once came into his office, saw a group of officials scurrying around, including an ambassador or two, and decided the signing of a treaty was imminent; so he took his seat at the head of the table and signed. On a less formal occasion in New York City, he invited a high British foreign office official, Sir Alexander Cadogan, to Radio City Music Hall to see the show. Afterward the two men went backstage, where, on an impulse, Stettinius asked Cadogan to explain the Dumbarton Oaks agreements on the United Nations to the Rockettes. Truman had to get Stettinius out of the State Department because by the existing constitutional arrangement for the presidential succession he was first in line. Therefore, after the San Francisco Conference he appointed him America's principal delegate to the United Nations, and Stettinius went to New York. With this new distinction, the retiring secretary asked for and received a four-motor airplane and an office in the White House.

His successor, Byrnes, did much better; whatever Byrnes's ambitions may have been, he was exceedingly intelligent, a hard worker, and a patriot. He was also very hostile to and suspicious of Russia. Truman had asked Byrnes to be secretary of state immediately after Roosevelt's death, and had waited only a decent interval to get Stettinius out. Byrnes was the obvious man for the post, as he had been to Yalta, where he took notes of the proceedings at the big round table (in his early years he had been a court reporter), and he had spent the war years in the White House as Roosevelt's assistant for domestic affairs. Before that he had enjoyed long service in the Senate and House of Representatives, having entered Congress at the beginning of the Wilson administration. Byrnes naturally felt he knew more about foreign affairs than Truman did, and it was said that he had told an aide in December 1945 at the Moscow Conference of foreign ministers that he would inform the president of proceedings in the Russian capital when he got good and ready. After his return to the United States, he asked immediately for radio time to discuss what had happened in Moscow. The president insisted that he come down to the yacht *Williamsburg*, cruising below Washington, and relate what had happened before announcing it to the nation. There is reason to believe that Truman told Byrnes off during that session, although, when the two men met in the White House early in the next month, the president may not have read to Byrnes the memorandum in which Truman said he was tired of "babying" the Russians and inferred that Byrnes had been doing so.

Despite an argument or two, the differences between the two men were more of style than of substance. Truman was not really ready for a tough policy in early 1946; he may only have been offended by Byrnes's failure to keep him informed, and he was slightly annoyed that Byrnes was attempting to take a "horse-trading" approach with the Soviets. Byrnes's many years in Congress had taught him how to talk to adversaries. Truman was no less a politician, but his approach was more direct.

Byrnes did well as secretary of state during the first year and a half of peace. He held office at an awkward time, when it was difficult to know what the Russians wanted and when about all an American secretary of state could have arranged were such minor issues as treaties of peace for the former Nazi satellites. Byrnes left in January 1947 for health reasons, but he later came into conflict again with the president, this time by moving toward the Dixiecrat camp—the antiblack Southerners who opposed Truman's nomination and election in 1948.

General Marshall, a man of vast experience with the highest military-political matters and a decisive man like his White House chief, succeeded Byrnes. Marshall and Truman had gotten along well ever since the occasion after Pearl Harbor when Colonel Truman had visited the chief of staff, and the affection had increased to such a point that Truman described Marshall as the greatest living American—even during the war, when another great American lived at the White House. Marshall's first undersecretary, Dean Acheson, found the general charming—as did the president.

In early 1947, when Marshall took over the State Department, he made a housekeeping decision that showed his decisiveness. Acheson told him that the department's offices had spilled out of the old State, War and Navy Building—an aging structure west of the White House—and that the department now had annexes all over the city. Acheson had discovered that a one-time War Department building was available in Foggy Bottom, a section of the city near the Potomac, and he wanted to move the department there. "Move," said Marshall.

Marshall could look at a problem, ask a few questions, inquire sharply if the right people had been consulted, and make up his mind. One of his favorite expressions was, "Don't fight the problem, solve it." Acheson had also been undersecretary to

Byrnes and had deplored the South Carolinian's complex calculations; to Acheson, Marshall was a breath of fresh air.

Acheson did not take office as Truman's fourth secretary of state until almost the end of the change in American foreign relations brought about by the Truman doctrine, the Marshall Plan, and NATO; he took over the department in January 1949, when Marshall resigned because of ill health. Acheson had been undersecretary in 1945–1947, and he was as much responsible as anyone for turning United States policy toward permanent participation in the affairs of Europe and the world. In Byrnes's time and during the first six months of Marshall's tenure, Acheson had been a driving force for change. He was acting secretary in 1946, during Byrnes's absence at meetings of the council of foreign ministers, and again early in 1947, when Marshall attended a council meeting in Moscow. Like Truman, he realized that occasional interventions in Europe and the Far East would not protect United States interests in the heated international atmosphere of the nuclear age against so powerful an antagonist as Soviet Russia, led by the implacable Stalin. Acheson was a tall, elegant lawyer, the son of an Episcopal bishop and a graduate of Groton, Yale, and Harvard Law School. He had been a clerk to Justice Brandeis, a member of the Washington firm of Covington and Burling, undersecretary of the treasury for a short time in 1933 (until he resigned over policy), assistant secretary of state commencing in 1941, and undersecretary beginning in August 1945. Acheson was born in Middletown, Connecticut, in the 1890s, and he fondly remembered the rural New England of his youth. Like Truman, he would have liked to have gone back to smalltown life, but he knew that it was impossible to return himself or national affairs back to turn-of-the-century ways, for two great wars had made the world a vastly different place.

Two other factors were effecting a change in American foreign relations—one military, the other economic. At the end of World War II, the great American military machine in Europe and Asia collapsed under the weight of public opinion that "the

boys," the men in the armed forces, had done their duty and
had every right to come home. As a result of this popular
pressure, a ruinous point system was conceived to disband the
military forces of the United States. The army and navy dis-
charged men according to points that were amassed—for each
month of service, each month abroad, service in particular battle
areas, and possession of a wife and children (an arrangement
that irritated unmarried veterans). A sort of musical chairs
followed, as the next-experienced men took their places. Before
long, the armed forces were in near-total confusion as hundreds
of thousands, then millions, departed. At the end of 1945 this
process of turning order into chaos, known grandly as demobilization, was not moving fast enough to suit those still in
uniform, and men rioted in Germany and the Far East. Wives
sent pictures of children to congressmen bearing the inscription,
"I want my Daddy," and thousands of booties with similarly
inscribed tags. Congressmen wrote letters to the military
departments predicting a terrible state of affairs if Sergeant So-
and-So did not go home. When General Eisenhower became
chief of staff in November 1945, his first task was to deal with
demobilization, and he assured Congress of his personal
attention to letters from aggrieved members of the armed
forces.

The primary embarrassment of demobilization for the Truman administration was that, in 1946 and 1947 and probably to
the beginning of the Korean War in June 1950, the United States
possessed no military forces capable of protecting Europe or the
Far East from a Soviet onslaught, short of the atomic bomb,
which the president privately refused to use. In a speech at the
Pentagon in November 1950, General Marshall recalled the state
of affairs—people pressing him "to give the Russians hell" and
making "the same appeal in relation to the Far East and China."
In 1947 his total forces for "giving hell" were one and a third
divisions over the entire United States. As he said, "This is quite
a proposition when you deal with somebody with over 260 and

you have 1⅓. We had nothing in Alaska. We did not have enough to defend the air strip at Fairbanks. . . . "

The dire economic situation in Europe also contributed to the change in American foreign relations. Great Britain was the dramatic case. In winter 1946–1947 a succession of the worst blizzards in many years descended on the British Isles, interspersed with bitter, unrelenting cold; snow and ice blocked roads, railways, rivers, and ships in port, isolated hundreds of communities, closed coal pits, killed winter wheat; the coal shortage became so acute that London went on four to five hours of electricity daily.

Matters were equally bad on the Continent. In France a severe drought killed most of the 1946 wheat crop; the cold destroyed between 3,200,000 and 3,800,000 acres of winter wheat, and the French were forced to import wheat at a hundred dollars a ton. Farmers refused to send supplies to the cities because the war had inflated the currency; they had almost nothing to sell anyway. In chilled urban areas, with food prices climbing, people were reaching the point at which they might accept any government that fed them and kept them warm. Communists were in cabinet posts, including the Ministry of Defense, and they appeared ready for a takeover. Italy had the same troubles.

Germany offered an abysmal economic picture, although the Western zones seemed safe because of the armies of occupation. Industrial production in early 1947 was 27 percent of prewar production. Reporting to Americans in late 1947, former President Hoover said that Germany's food supplies had sunk to a level not known in the Western world for a hundred years. Hoover wanted to send over ten million tons of American potatoes, because farmers at home had so many they were using them for fertilizer, but the Germans had no money, and the U.S. Department of Agriculture judged the potatoes low-grade and hence inedible. In 1936 Germany produced 85 percent of its food; in 1947 it produced 25 percent. Population in the Western-occupied zones was nine million more than in 1939, increased by refugees from overrun areas in the East. Many of the refugees were women, children, and old people, who were not productive and only added to the need for food. Manpower was scarce because more than three million prisoners remained in Russia.

Europeans had no money with which to purchase American goods. The United States made a huge loan to the British in 1946—$3.75 billion—but it hardly sufficed, and a large part of it immediately began to go out to the British zone of Germany to "feed the damned Germans," as Chancellor of the Exchequer Hugh Dalton put it.

In a famous speech in May 1947, Churchill declared that Europe was "a rubble-heap, a charnel house, a breeding-ground of pestilence and hate." A later writer remarked: "Like a whale left gasping on the sand, Europe lay rotting in the sun."

In early 1947, a crisis arose in Eastern Europe over Greece and Turkey; the problem was what to do with those two nations when the British stopped supporting them. Greece had been a British preserve for many years, and the British army had returned in late 1944 when the Germans had retreated, leaving the country wrecked economically and confused politically. Seven changes of government within two years after liberation did not improve matters; Athens politicians shuttled in and out of power. The Greek Communist party began to organize guerrilla bands in the mountains in the summer of 1946. The government's foreign exchange reserves disappeared. The prospective deficit of the Greek government for 1947 was nearly $300 million—three times the currency in circulation. A flaming inflation presaged economic collapse.

Turkey's troubles were less critical but similar. The British had also given subsidies to Turkey, an independent-minded nation that had a poor economy but maintained a large army against the Russian troops ranged along its borders. At the end of World War II, the Soviets began to push the Turks for unconditional transit rights in the Dardanelles, and asked for the return of provinces lost to Turkey during the Russian revolution.

There was evidence that the Soviets were seeking to make Turkey into a satellite.

The British did not want to drop either Greece or Turkey in American laps, but they were not economically able to continue their subsidies. Early in 1947, a representative of the British embassy in Washington came to the State Department and informed the duty officer that, in the spring, the British would have to cease their support of Greece and Turkey.

The American response was the Truman Doctrine, announced by the president to a joint session of Congress on March 12, 1947, in the form of a recommendation to send $400 million to Greece and Turkey to protect them against communism. The Truman Doctrine amounted to a declaration against Russian influence beyond the boundaries laid down in 1945.

The general nature of the doctrine—unspecific limits—was based on a calculation by Undersecretary Acheson, to whom the Department of State's speechwriter, Joseph M. Jones, went for advice on Truman's speech to Congress. Acheson leaned back from his desk, looked over at the White House, thought a while, and said slowly, "If F.D.R. were alive I think I know what he'd do. He would make a statement of global policy but confine his request for money right now to Greece and Turkey." During debate on the appropriation in Congress, Representative Walter H. Judd of Minnesota, former medical missionary to China and a hard-line Republican, raised the issue of China and asked why it was necessary to combat communism in Greece and Turkey when American policy in China was to unite the Nationalists of Chaing Kai-shek and the Communists of Mao Tse-tung into one government. Acheson tried to tell Judd and the Republicans that China was forty-five times as large as Greece, its population eighty-five times as large, but Judd did not want that sort of logic.

A year after Churchill's speech at Westminster College the president had reason to oppose Communist pressure in the Eastern Mediterranean, but his pronouncement about two small countries on the eastern fringe of Europe did not resolve the economic crisis in Western Europe. No sooner had the administration decided on its Russian policy than a new decision was necessary on a program to stop economic disintegration. The old way of dealing with Europe no longer worked. The United States had given great sums to the United Nations Relief and Rehabilitation Administration (UNRRA), which disbursed them as poor relief. The methods of disbursement bothered many Americans, who believed that the origin of the funds was not made clear to recipients; and Communists used UNRRA money to back their rule in Eastern Europe. Meanwhile, the United States had made grants to the military government in Germany to cope with problems there. The 1946 loan to the British had met with difficulty in Congress, where members argued that it supported the empire, and loans to other governments were bound to be more difficult. Economic crisis would allow Communists into coalition governments, however, as was already the case in France, and it was feared that the hungry, cold Europeans would soon heed the siren call from the East.

The man who first advocated the Marshall Plan in 1947 was Undersecretary of State William L. Clayton, an experienced observer, whose firm, Anderson, Clayton and Company, was the world's largest cotton merchant. Clayton came back from a quick tour of Europe appalled by what he had seen, and he described it to Marshall in graphic terms. Marshall then talked to the president. Acheson announced the new American program in a speech in Mississippi in May 1947; Marshall also announced it in a speech at Harvard commencement in early June.

The need at the outset was for a program of interim aid, because time was running out in Europe: countries needed dollar exchange immediately. The UNRRA, to which the United States had contributed liberally, came to an end that spring of 1947, when American taxpayers balked at contributing to an agency they could not control. Congress then passed appropriations for interim aid until the Marshall Plan was organized.

Getting the program under way required European nations to make a proposal to the United States—and Marshall wanted a joint proposal, not various shopping lists. When the proposal came in, late in August, for about $29 billion spread over four years, he trimmed it to $17.8 billion and divided it into smaller amounts to make it more acceptable to Congress and the American people. After a large educational campaign that involved complex analysis by public and official committees, Congress passed the first fifteen-month appropriation for $6.8 billion, and the president signed it on April 3, 1948. When Marshall Plan appropriations came to an end in 1952, they had run to $13,348,800,000.

At the time, many Americans believed the Marshall Plan might bankrupt the United States. Thirteen billion dollars was no small sum, and it surely added to the national debt, which by then was $250 billion. The cost was easily bearable at the time, however. An inquiry into the statistics of American consumption showed a domestic liquor bill of more than $13 billion, a tobacco bill of more than that, and an athletic bill of far more. The economy had plenty of slack. The appropriations were well below the cost of the wartime lend-lease of over $50 billion, and they were well below the cost of the Korean War. Americans could congratulate themselves that, because of the Marshall Plan, they did not have to pay for another enormous war in Europe.

The Marshall Plan came at the right time to allow Western Europe to take advantage of the economic boom caused by the Korean War, which began when the plan was ending and brought huge war orders to Europe. The Marshall Plan and the war orders took Europeans into a consumer-oriented economy such as the Americans had entered in the 1920s.

American foreign relations thus changed in 1947–1949, first with a declaration of principle—the Truman Doctrine—then by providing an economic foundation through the Marshall Plan that allowed Western Europe to avoid coalition governments with Communists and to escape the danger of passing behind the iron curtain. The third measure that changed American foreign relations was the North Atlantic Treaty Organization (NATO).

The NATO alliance created a military buffer around the peoples of Western Europe. The need for such a buffer became apparent in 1948. There was no point in supporting Europe economically and then having it fall to a military attack from the East European satellite nations or the Soviet Union. The United States already had a core of four divisions in the West Germany occupation forces, but the Berlin blockade that began in June 1948 and continued until May 1949 raised the issue of a need for a Western military organization. The Truman administration hesitated about NATO, lest it seem provocative to the Soviets. It was a difficult period in domestic politics, also. Truman was running for his political life against the Republican candidate, Governor Dewey, and he could do little about NATO unless he won the election. Discussions had been going on quietly, however, and began to move forward in November. On April 4, 1949, Secretary of State Acheson signed the North Atlantic Treaty in Washington with the two signatories of the Treaty of Dunkirk of 1947—Britain and France—joined by the Benelux countries (Belgium, the Netherlands, and Luxembourg), which, with the British and French, had signed the Brussels Pact of 1948. The NATO alliance included three countries to the north—Iceland, Denmark, and Norway—but not traditionally neutral Sweden. It also included Portugal, the long-time ally of Britain, but not Spain, because Generalissimo Francisco Franco was still very much alive and in power. Italy, the former enemy, was also included. In 1952 the countries guaranteed support by the Truman Doctrine—Greece and Turkey, at the eastern end of the Mediterranean—came in, because the Korean War clearly showed the danger to countries that were excluded from America's defense perimeter. Three years later, the West Germans joined, as a preliminary to their attainment of full sovereignty that year.

The NATO organization existed only on paper in 1949 and had no troops other than those already in the occupation forces of the United States, Britain, and France, together with a few battalions maintained by the Benelux countries and other members. For nearly two years it showed little ability to organize further. In January 1951, President Truman sent General Eisenhower to Europe and, at the Lisbon Conference of 1952, NATO adopted a plan for a hundred divisions, with fifty ready at any time. The Lisbon goals were never reached; after West Germany joined in the mid-1950s, only half the planned number of divisions were on the line. Whatever its weaknesses, however, NATO did present a point of resistance to an eastern enemy, preventing the possibility of an attack by the Soviet satellites that might not appear serious at first but could infiltrate Western Europe. The NATO presence provided enough resistance to alert its membership, especially the United States, so that they could deal with attackers through diplomacy or war. Moreover, NATO's existence eased the fears of West Europeans, allowing them the freedom to plan their economic futures.

By contrast with past feelings of indifference, the Truman administration and the people of the United States now recognized that Europe's distress was America's distress. Truman had radically changed the nation's foreign policy.

The word that best describes the change is probably *containment*—the drawing of a line around the Soviet Union and its satellites in Eastern Europe so as to set off the borders of communism from those of what was loosely described in 1947 and thereafter as the free world. George F. Kennan, the first head of the State Department's policy planning staff when it was organized in 1947, often was credited as the author of this new doctrine. Kennan had nothing to do with the Truman Doctrine, but he did contribute to formulation of the Marshall Plan. He also had little to do with NATO. His principal contribution to containment was an essay, "The Sources of Soviet Conduct," published in mid-1947 in the journal *Foreign Affairs* under the pseudonym "Mr. X." The article stated that the sources of conduct were ideology and circumstances, the ideal and the real, theory and opportunity. It was written with entrancing style, and its excursions into Russian history gave it broad currency. Although his essay was read and reread by a generation of literate Americans, Kennan was a minor figure among the leaders in containment. The president himself was foremost in turning policy against further Russian expansion, and Marshall and Acheson backed him up, supported by Clayton and the State Department's other major Russian expert, Charles Bohlen, who had been Roosevelt's interpreter at Yalta and, like Kennan, turned to Russian studies at the end of the 1920s, becoming expert long before wartime and postwar shifts in relations.

Afterward, containment seemed more logical, more planned, than was actually the case. First had come the idea, the Truman Doctrine; then the economic plan; then the scholarly rationale; then the military alliance. But events did not move so steadily. The transition often was slow and plodding and, in the case of NATO, awaited a national election a year and a half after the Truman Doctrine.

Containment in itself was not a novel doctrine. It really traced back to the idea of collective security—the basic notion of the League of Nations of 1919, the idea that only in community might nations flourish or even survive. Containment had unilateral aspects in both the Truman Doctrine and the Marshall Plan, but the latter included all interested nations of Western Europe, and those nations had to present their economic proposals as a plan. The culmination was the NATO alliance, with its concept of "all for one, one for all," which was in essence an institution for collective security. In NATO's later years, the 1970s and 1980s, it turned its attention to mutual decreases of armaments between East and West. Thus, NATO was not a fortress but, rather, was one of the instruments, as Kennan put it, for negotiation and protection.

Mistakes were made in the transition to containment, and people pointed them out at the time and later. In announcing the Truman Doctrine, the president had allowed his speechwriter, Joe Jones, to compose a speech that was too strenuous, too hardline. He did this on the advice of Senator Vandenberg, who allegedly had told him to scare hell out of the country. Jones set up a crisis that did not exist, though it might have emerged later: he depicted the evil men of the Kremlin waiting to pounce on a weak America. Part of the trouble with the speech was Jones's imitation of the president's prose, wherein each sentence marched in platoon fashion from subject to verb to object; the speech had no flair, and it read like legal testimony. Later—when people realized that the Russians were not ten feet tall and, as in the Cuban missile crisis of 1962, were weaker than the Americans—the Truman Doctrine's prose, including all Jones's "shoulds" that Truman changed to his own "musts," seemed exaggerated. Still, Truman took a stand in a way reminiscent of Roosevelt, with a grand statement and a small appropriation. He laid down a principle and within weeks sponsored a serious economic program and then NATO.

In the first months of 1948, the Russians made a series of moves that resulted, on June 24, in a complete land blockade of the three Western sectors of Berlin—American, British, and French. The former German capital occupied a large area, spreading out for a dozen miles in all directions from its center at the Brandenburg gate, with the Soviet sector, almost half the city, to the east. The immediate problem for the Western nations became twofold: to feed their sectors' 2,250,000 Berliners and, both for industry and for warmth, to supply them with coal. At first the very idea of an airlift seemed impossible when President Truman announced it, for coal was a bulky, dirty fuel, not easy to carry by plane. By October 1948, the average daily airlift haul approached 5,000 tons, and when the Berlin blockade ended on May 12, it had proved a great success, a peaceful demonstration of Western ingenuity and power. The avowed Soviet purpose in starting the blockade had been to halt the Western currency reform, begun early in June 1948. The currency reform rekindled economic life within the Western zones, ending the increasing economic hardship that was threatening to turn all

Western Europe toward communism. Together with participation in the Marshall Plan, currency reform in West Germany brought the *Wirtschaftswunder*, the economic wonder of German industrial revival in the late 1940s. When the blockade failed in 1949, the Soviets ended it without stopping the introduction of the new currency into West Berlin. They thereby showed that their real purpose in the blockade probably had been to halt the execution of the so-called London Recommendations of June 1948—the planned introduction of self-rule in the Western zones of Germany, which led in 1949 to the establishment of a West German government in Bonn.

In August 1949, the Russians exploded a nuclear device, an event that, like the Berlin blockade of 1948–1949, was unnerving to the West. At first, Truman refused to believe that the Soviets had acquired the technology for a bomb, although, by this time, he understood that there was no bomb secret and that they probably had the know-how anyway, for all top nuclear physicists could elaborate theoretical ways to produce a bomb. His advisers had thought that the Soviets would need much more time than the four years they took—the same time required by the Manhattan Project. This event prompted the decision to construct a superbomb, the hydrogen implosion (rather than explosion) weapon called the H-bomb, which required a so-called atomic bomb as a trigger. In September 1949, the president quietly allotted $300 million to the Atomic Energy Commission. This was the decisive step, preceding his public announcement of the new project on January 31, 1950.

Here again, in the decision to go ahead with the H-bomb, the president probably made a mistake. Many years later, a critic pointed out that Truman had faced a poor choice. His advisers on one side had argued that, if he held off developing the H-bomb, the Russians would get one first and then blackmail the United States in ways it never had experienced in its history. On the other hand, advisers such as Robert Oppenheimer, the wartime director of the Los Alamos nuclear weapons laboratory, and President James B. Conant of Harvard argued that, if the

United States did not develop the H-bomb, the Soviets might also hold back. The new weapon, they claimed correctly, was immoral: it could not be aimed, and it would escalate warfare indefinitely, depending only on the megatonnage of new bombs. They had no answer to the possibility of Soviet black-mail. To risk such a chance, of course, was highly imprudent during the Stalin era, and Truman therefore opted for the new weapon. McGeorge Bundy, the former national security adviser of the early 1960s, later argued that there had been a third course—a proposal of forebearance—offering the Soviet Union a treaty ban on all H-bomb testing. The ban could have been enforced by atmospheric sampling and did not require on-site inspection. In the rush of public business during the immediate postwar years, this opportunity, set out by Bundy in retrospect, was lost; in 1949–1950, with the H-bomb decision, the nuclear arms race escalated dangerously.

Not all problems of foreign policy at this time concerned Soviet Russia. One of them, which dealt with the Middle East rather than with Europe, was the Palestine issue. Creation of the State of Israel was resisted by the State Department but championed in the executive offices by Clark M. Clifford and David K. Niles, Truman's counsel and his assistant for minor-ities, respectively. The new nation came into existence in May 1948, with the support of Jewish Americans. The idea of a national home for Jews had come out of the Balfour Declaration of 1917, a casual pronouncement by the British foreign secre-tary, Lord Balfour, that looked vaguely toward a Jewish state in the area of Palestine. After World War I, the British had accepted a Palestine mandate and had done little more about a Jewish national home than allow immigration until, in 1939, that policy became nearly impossible because of Arab opposition. A British white paper that year reduced immigration to 75,000 over the next five years, a totally unrealistic figure that en-couraged illegal immigration. With the end of World War II, the lid came off in Palestine. Jews and Arabs fought each other and in 1947, the year of Britain's retreat from Greece and Turkey and

also from India, the British gave Palestine to the United Nations.
The United Nations opted for two national regimes in Palestine,
Jewish and Arab, and the British set a date for their own
departure—May 15, 1948. The question then became one of
boundaries, and the Jews determined to establish their own.
Truman tired of the controversy, especially Jewish pressure
during the General Assembly decision of November 1947. After
his old haberdashery partner, Eddie Jacobson, beseeched him
to receive the future president of Israel, Chaim Weizmann, who
was visiting in New York, the president relented, and he told
Weizmann that the United States would not intervene. In March
1948, the State Department proposed a great-power trusteeship,
without telling the president, and Truman claimed that it was
the work of "people on the 3rd and 4th levels of the State Dept.
who have always wanted to cut my throat. They've succeeded in
doing it." The problem righted itself for the Jews with the Israeli
proclamation of independence on May 14, 1948, at 6:00 P.M.
Washington time, midnight in Tel Aviv. Official American
recognition came quickly, at 6:11 P.M., to the embarrassment of
the American United Nations delegates, who at that very
moment were arguing trusteeship. The president does not seem
to have thought of potential problems; he believed that recognition was the right decision. Advocates of Israeli independence
argued that it created a friendly state in the Middle East and that,
after the holocaust, the Jews deserved a country. Opponents
argued that, in one fell swoop, the Truman administration had
ruined chances for peace in the Middle East. The president had
perhaps given his reasoning a year and a half before, when,
speaking to a group of American diplomats working in the
Middle East, he said, "I'm sorry, gentlemen, but I have to
answer to hundreds of thousands who are anxious for the
success of Zionism; I do not have hundreds of thousands of
Arabs among my constituents."

Another non-Soviet, non-European problem of the time was
what to do with the small countries known as the Third World
that were clamoring for aid from the United States. Even before

passage of the Marshall Plan appropriations there was constant talk in Latin America about the United States establishing an economic plan for the western hemisphere. This talk rose to a high pitch of insistence in 1947, when, at a conference in Rio de Janeiro, the United States managed a security pact among the Latin American republics. The Rio Pact went into effect in December 1948, and eventually all twenty-one signatories ratified it. The pact provided for mandatory economic and optional military measures in case of a dangerous "fact or situation," but it said nothing about economic aid. Asian countries also were inquiring about aid. The result was a program presented in Truman's inaugural address of 1949, known as Point IV, that promised technical assistance. In subsequent years, it received small appropriations, becoming more a promise than a program.

For President Truman, the postwar years beginning in 1947 were a time of problem after problem, with some successes and some failures. He handled every problem as well as he could. There was always something to do, however, and busyness sometimes got in the way of thought. There was a constant swirl of visitors, many meetings at which he had to make statements, a frequent need to make speeches, and regular dealings with the hordes of newspaper correspondents who besieged the White House looking for news whether it was there or not. Their wartime experience had accustomed the American people to expect news every day, usually in the evening at suppertime, and correspondents provided it for newspapers or radio stations. Beginning in 1950, they provided it for television as well. Truman had to respond to these expectations, in the hope that he might inform the American people and get them to vote the Democratic ticket and choose good leaders.

Something was always going on; it was a terribly busy time. In March 1947, the Senate argued about confirming David Lilienthal as chairman of the Atomic Energy Commission, because it did not like his actions as chairman of the Tennessee Valley Authority, where he had championed public ownership of power plants. Senators talked of socialism, equating it with communism, and the president wrote in a memorandum he did not release: "If Mr. L. is a Communist so am I."

The president was a hardworking, basically cheerful man, a believer in his country. When a problem arose, he solved it if he could. This was how he had handled the business of his Senate committee and before that the committee investigating the railroads, the county court in Independence, Battery D of the 129th Field Artillery, the Grandview farm, and the National Bank of Commerce of Kansas City. In the years after 1945, the main issue he had to deal with was the Soviet Union. He did the best he could, and, as he wrote Vivian Truman at one point when pressure was heavy, "The things go up and down—one day you do things you think are for the welfare of the country and the next you are up against a complete reversal of feeling because something else that is right doesn't please. I think the proper thing to do, and the thing I have been doing, is to do what I think is right and let them all go to hell."

Inauguration, 1949

V

To Err Is Truman

IN DOMESTIC AFFAIRS the end of the war brought an awkward adjustment to peace and, almost automatically, the troubles of the time—economic, social, political—focused on the president of the United States. Truman's popularity plummeted, and nothing he did sufficed to make critics feel he was equal to the office of president. The critics did not remember that the American Revolution had been followed by such turmoil as to lead to a new Constitution, that the Civil War had produced hatreds that had lasted until the turn of the century, that economic dislocation and the "red scare" that had followed World War I had bedeviled President Wilson. It was Truman's misfortune to hold the presidency after the victories in Europe and Japan, when the country's problems would have tested any leader.

An Indian summer of political peace had lasted until the Japanese surrender on August 14, 1945. Then the troubles began, first over price controls. During the war, the Office of Price Administration (OPA) had sought to control eight million commodities and services through both rationing and price controls. It produced a new currency—red, green, and other ration stamps—without which no one could buy much. The OPA also set prices. Most Americans went along with the program, and its success was evident in the fact that consumer prices rose only 30 percent over 1939 levels; in World War I, without rationing and price controls, prices had more than doubled. At the end of the war, however, the pent-up personal savings in banks and government bonds threatened to pass into personal consumption. Production had risen from $101.4 billion in 1940 to $215.2 billion in 1945. In 1945 the level of savings was astronomical—$136.4 billion. Orderly deregulation of consumption was in almost everyone's interest, to prevent pent-up demand from exploding into inflation—too many dollars chasing too few goods. Anyone who had saved was bound to get into trouble as his dollars inflated, unless he got them out of the bank or bonds and put them into real estate or perhaps stock—something to express the inflating dollar. Labor unions were bound to strike, as employers moved as slowly as possible to avoid wage increases and to pocket the difference between the cost of their goods and the prices they received. Inflation would trap anyone on a fixed income.

Rationing went out with the end of the war, and many businessmen and consumers demanded an immediate end to price controls, too. They argued that, because of the American tradition of free enterprise and individual initiative, the proper course was to take off all regulations. They spoke of needless shortages, failing to remark that, as soon as war ended, businessmen sensed the advantage in holding their wares until prices went up. Because the veritable army of 78,000 local price-control regulators was disintegrating from natural causes at the end of the war, when many of them gave up their jobs, it was difficult to police the postwar OPA system—another reason the critics used to urge the end of regulations.

Congress finally voted to continue OPA, but the resultant bill mangled the authority of the office. Truman vetoed the bill, and price controls ended at midnight, June 30, 1946. Prices rose rapidly: veal cutlets from fifty to ninety-five cents a pound, milk from sixteen to twenty cents a quart. Consumers rebelled, and Congress got the message and enacted a new, flimsier price-control bill and Truman signed it. The gap in enforcement wrecked price-control machinery, however. A meat shortage followed, and the Republicans said they would take off controls on beef after the election in November 1946, which they clearly were going to win. Truman abandoned the price line, however, and the OPA became known, in the irreverent words of its last administrator, Paul A. Porter, as the Office for Cessation of Rationing and Priorities—OCRAP.

No other single problem of the postwar domestic economy so consumed the time of President Truman as did price controls. The Republicans were magnificently irrelevant, simply ignoring the issue. At the height of the furor over meat prices, reporters asked one of the most influential GOP leaders in the upper house, Senator Robert A. Taft of Ohio, for his solution; his answer was "Eat less." The assumption, fit only for the eighteenth century, before industry, cities, world wars, and shortages, was that Americans solved their problems without government. Truman received conflicting advice from his old friend, Secretary of the Treasury John W. Snyder, and the wartime head of the OPA, Chester Bowles. The trouble was that neither a conservative nor a liberal solution for the OPA was right. Only patience was right, and no one, least of all the president, had any. Truman blamed the American people for selfishness and greed. In October 1946, he wrote out a bitter speech, which he decided not to deliver and filed away, but it showed his feelings. He accused the people of having "forgotten the ideals for which we fought under Franklin Roosevelt. . . . You would sacrifice the greatest government that was ever conceived in the mind of man for a mess of pottage—for a piece of beef, for a slice of bacon." Selfish industrialists and labor leaders who gave up nothing to win the war wanted to profit from "the blood and sacrifice of the brave men who bared their breasts to the bullets." He would no longer enforce a law "botched and bungled by an unwilling Congress." Here was the low point of Truman's presidency. He was an ebullient man not given to pessimism, ready to look at the sunny side of life, not easy to "get down." At the end of his speech he wrote a final line: "Tell 'em what will happen and quit."

In this draft speech, as he thought of resigning, the president mentioned not only businessmen, who had things to sell, but labor leaders, whose actions constituted another side of the coin in 1946, a year marked by strikes. When the new year opened, 900,000 workers were out, led by the auto workers, followed by 700,000 steel workers, 263,000 packinghouse workers, 200,000 electrical workers, and 50,000 communications workers. The year registered 116 million days of work lost to strikes, three times higher than ever before. Considering that the nation had more than 60 million workers in 1946, it was not a tremendous number of days lost, but it was a great many for crucial industries, two of which, bituminous coal and the railroads, required weeks of presidential time as Truman attempted to get men back to work and end the grave danger of a collapse of the economy.

John L. Lewis, shaggy veteran of years of labor fights, led the miners' union, and they went out for forty days until, on May 21, 1946, the president signed an order seizing the mines. Coal provided more than half of all industrial energy and electric power. Before the complete conversion of locomotives to diesel power, before great fleets of trucks filled the nation's highways, and before development of commercial air traffic, coal was extremely important for moving freight and passengers. After the seizure of the mines, the president gave concessions to the miners. Everything seemed to have been settled, but then Lewis seized on a technicality in the contract with the government and asked to reopen the whole negotiation. When Secretary of the Interior Krug refused, Lewis said the miners would cancel their contract, and "no contract, no work." All this blew up inconveniently in October 1946, just before the congressional elections. Truman was furious and told his press secretary, Charlie Ross, that this time he would "go to the mat with Lewis." The head of the miners' union bided his time through the elections, and so did the president, and in mid-November the president decided to use an injunction against the miners, raising one of the ancient grievances of laboring men. The Norris-LaGuardia Act of 1932 and Wagner Act of 1935 had outlawed such behavior by employers, but had not foreseen a situation in which the government would be the employer. The government served the injunction on November 18, and a judge cited Lewis and the miners' union for contempt of court. After the trial, which opened early in December, the judge fined the union $3.5 million and Lewis personally $10,000—the stiffest penalties ever imposed in a case of labor contempt. It looked as if Lewis would go to jail, which would solve nothing, because the country would be unable to mine coal without the miners; but Lewis caved in and the men went back to work.

In the early part of the argument with the miners, another great strike was threatened by the two railroad brotherhoods led by Alexander F. Whitney and Alvanley Johnston. The issue was personally embarrassing to the president; he had won reelection to the Senate in 1940 partly because Johnston had marshaled the Missouri railroad unions in his support. Labor had generally been friendly to Truman, and his nomination for the vice-presidency had had its fervent support. It was one thing to take a stand against Lewis of the United Mine Workers, a cantankerously independent fellow, and quite another to oppose Whitney and Johnston, statesmen in the labor movement. Everything came down to a crisis: eighteen of the twenty railroad brotherhoods went along with a settlement on the basis of an arbitrated award, but not Whitney and Johnston. Truman called the recalcitrants to his office on May 15, 1946, and spoke in his frank manner: "If you think I'm going to sit here and let you tie up this whole country," said the president of the United States, "you're crazy as hell."

"We've got to go through with it, Mr. President," said Whitney. "Our men are demanding it." Truman got up from his desk. "All right," he said, "I'm going to give you the gun. You've got just 48 hours—until Thursday at this time—to reach a settlement. If you don't I'm going to take over the railroads in the name of the government."

The crisis spun on until Saturday, May 25, 1946, when the president was making a rousing speech before Congress relating what the government needed to do, including a proposal to draft strikers into the army. In the middle of the speech, an aide passed a note up to him; he looked it over, grinned, and said, "Gentlemen, the strike has been settled." He went through with the speech, and the House of Representatives passed a striker-draft recommendation with a whoop. The Senate defeated it.

In retrospect, the president's position on the railroad strike was understandable as the action of the nation's chief executive, who did not want the entire economy tied up by a small group of strikers out for their own advantage. It was awkward, however, for Truman to threaten to draft strikers into the army; this could hardly be considered democracy in action. Civil rights and liberties were involved, for the railroad workers surely needed protection against military discipline. What Truman proposed in 1946 would have been analogous to President Ronald Reagan's drafting the striking air traffic controllers in 1981. Regardless of sentiment throughout the country, reflected in the House of Representatives, the country might have been better off in 1946 if Truman had not advocated a striker draft. Although the president did not have to go through with it, he passed on to future generations a proposal contrary to the actions of preceding presidents and to the Constitution that produced the presidency.

The strikes of 1946 inspired Congress to revise the statutes relating to unions, and Truman vetoed the first revision, the Case Bill of June 1946. Congress passed the less extreme Taft-Hartley Bill a year later, over his veto. The new enactment outlawed industry-wide strikes, closed shops, and mass picketing; made unions liable to suits; required union leaders to file noncommunist affidavits before they could use the facilities of the National Labor Relations Board; set up cooling-off periods before strikes; prohibited use of union funds for political contributions; and gave the president power to obtain injunctions in strikes involving interstate commerce, public utilities, and communications.

The period after World War II was a time of trouble for the Democratic party. The collapse of the OPA and the bitter strikes in major industries in 1946 weakened Truman's reputation with the voters, even though no president in American history had talked so roughly to union leaders. It was especially easy to be critical of the new man in the White House. The transition from the "dazzling Hyde Park patrician" to the gray little county judge from Independence evoked talk of power shifting from the Hudson to the Missouri. Perhaps that was to the good— Kansas City was not far from the geographical center of the United States, and the Hudson was a mere stream compared with the Missouri. But many Easterners talked of a "Missouri compromise."

The president's appointees also came in for criticism. At first, the critics said, the Truman appointees seemed funny rather than dangerous: they were not putting their hands in the till because they were too busy putting their feet in their mouths. In a book entitled *The Truman Merry-Go-Round*, two Washington syndicated columnists asserted that the White House staff was a bunch of political stumblebums, a collection of weary, faceless hacks. "The mere announcement in April, 1945, that Harry Truman was President flushed them out of every dark cove and secluded thicket." Criticism extended to anyone working for the government. A later *Wall Street Journal* cartoon caught the mood of 1945–1946; it showed a psychiatrist telling a nervous young man, "You need a rest. You need a government job."

Not since the administration of John Tyler had the American public cherished fewer illusions about the group in power in Washington, wrote Gerald W. Johnson, who was trying to defend the administration; hardly a day passed, he said, without a volley of criticism. People repeated silly things, such as the affair of a Washington influence peddler, Colonel James V. Hunt, who did have influence with the chief of the army chemical corps and the quartermaster general. Truman retired the first general and suspended the second, but the uproar continued. Newspapers made much of the fact that Colonel Hunt possessed matchboxes labeled "Swiped from Harry S. Truman." A matchbox manufacturer revealed that Hunt had ordered the matchboxes from him, but no one paid attention.

In 1946, the Republican party received from the Harry M. Frost Advertising Company of Boston a two-word slogan for the congressional elections that year: "Had enough?" The president appeared to have lost control of Congress, with its nominal Democratic majorities in both houses, to the southern conservative Democrats, who dominated the committees because of their seniority; and they had cemented their authority by voting frequently with northern and western conservative Republicans. Of the twenty-one legislative recommendations Truman submitted to Congress at the beginning of the 1946 session, the president lost thirteen, won about half of what he asked on two others, and secured six in the form he requested them. A critical reporter observed that it was a batting average of .333—good in baseball but not in government. Seeking to improve the prospects for the elections, the Democratic national committee played FDR's speech recordings in radio advertisements and consigned Truman to oblivion. In 1946, the nation elected a Republican Eightieth Congress; it was the first time the Republicans had won majorities in both houses in eighteen years.

President Truman did not seem to have a chance of election to the presidency in his own right in 1948. Everything conspired against him. His firing of Secretary of the Interior Harold L. Ickes in early 1946 (see Chapter IX) gathered disaffection in Democratic ranks; Democrats said Truman was not a New Dealer, even if during his years in the Senate he had supported Roosevelt down the line. Ickes's firing proved to liberal Democrats that the new president did not understand the old progressive-New Deal liberalism that Ickes symbolized. Not long afterward came a break with Secretary of Commerce Henry Wallace (see Chapter IX), Truman's antagonist at the Chicago convention of 1944. After Wallace resigned from the cabinet, he soon produced what Truman feared—a third party for the disaffected New Dealers. Ickes was an old man in 1946 and was not available for the presidency, but Wallace was in the prime of life and had been a large figure in the Roosevelt administration.

Wallace became editor of the *New Republic*, where he elaborated
startling ideas. "My field," he said, "is the world. My strength is
my conviction that a progressive America can unify the world
and a reactionary American must divide it." He opposed the
Truman Doctrine and the Marshall Plan because they were anti-
Soviet; to him, Big Three unity was essential. He announced his
candidacy in December 1947, and he welcomed support from
the American Communist party, which was quickly forth-
coming. The new party, which sought to capture the memories
of Theodore Roosevelt in 1912 and Robert M. La Follette in
1924, called itself the Progressive party. The choice, its keynote
speaker announced in 1948, was Wallace or war. As Roosevelt's
party of 1912 had marched around a hall in Chicago singing
"Onward Christian Soldiers," so the Wallaceites sang "The
Battle Hymn of the Republic":

> From the Bay of Massachusetts
> Out into the Golden Gate
> Henry Wallace leads his army
> 'Gainst destruction, fear and hate.
> We Americans will save the
> Precious land that we create
> For the people's march is on.
>
> Glory, glory, hallelujah . . .

More dangerous to Truman's election, indeed dangerous to
his nomination, was a boomlet for General Eisenhower's candidacy in the spring of 1948, when the general retired as chief of
staff of the U.S. Army. Eisenhower's politics were uncertain; he
had never even voted. Years later, Eisenhower related in his
memoirs that, at the end of World War II, President Truman
had proposed him as the Democratic nominee in 1948 but had
gone back on the proposition. Truman denied he had made
such an offer. The argument erupted in the 1960s, long after the
two men had become estranged. The truth rested on two
memories. When he met Eisenhower at Antwerp in July 1945,
just before the Potsdam Conference, Truman may have said

there was nothing he would not do for the American military hero "and that definitely includes the presidency in 1948." Harry Vaughan remembered a 1946 luncheon at the Pentagon, where, amid the banter, Truman joked, "General, if you ever decide you want to get into politics, you come to me and I'll endorse you." Secretary of the Army Kenneth Royall recalled that Truman had sent him to Eisenhower in 1947 to ask if Ike would run for the presidency, with Truman as his vice-presidential nominee. In any event, early in 1948, Eisenhower thwarted an effort by the Republicans to enter his name in the New Hampshire primary. Disaffected Democrats, led by President Roosevelt's son James (then a member of the House of Representatives from California) took the New Hampshire statement to mean that Ike would run on the Democratic ticket and pushed to commit him. Just before the Democratic convention, Jimmy Roosevelt persuaded eighteen other prominent party leaders to send a telegram to each of the 1,592 delegates to the convention, urging them to come to Philadelphia two days early to select "the ablest and strongest man available" as the party's candidate. Eisenhower probably was not interested; he was drifting into Republicanism because of his Kansas upbringing and his dislike of Democratic fiscal policy—a fear, as he expressed in his diary, that the federal government would spend itself into bankruptcy. He waited an appallingly long time, however, until two days before the convention, before issuing a pronouncement: "I would refuse to accept the nomination under any conditions, terms, or promises." The Democrats assembled in Philadelphia in a spirit of helpless gloom. "We're just Mild About Harry," read the convention signs.

Meanwhile, the president's position on the rights of black Americans produced another split in Democratic ranks. Truman's commitment to black rights went back to the unsegregated ways of Independence, Missouri, where, in the midst of a "lily-white" state, the blacks of the little town lived next to the whites and there were no problems. During his campaign for reelection to the Senate in 1940, Truman had courted black support, which proved to be a major factor in his narrow victory in the primary. A few months after he took office as president, when the Daughters of the American Revolution refused to permit the black pianist Hazel Scott, wife of Representative Adam Clayton Powell of New York, to appear in Constitution Hall, the president wrote a letter affirming that artistic talent was not the exclusive property of any race or group and that a mark of democracy was the willingness to respect and reward talent without regard to race or origin. Privately, Truman was furious with Powell, who had sent a telegram urging Mrs. Truman not to attend a DAR tea; Truman felt that the congressman had no business telling "the Madam" what to do. But his private displeasure did not become public. Late in 1946, he established a Committee on Civil Rights, under Charles E. Wilson of General Electric, to help him plan a program. In October 1947, the commission submitted its report, "To Secure These Rights," but the cabinet split badly over asking Congress to enact it. On February 2, 1948, without conferring with congressional leaders, the president sent to Congress a ten-point civil rights message calling for a strengthening of civil rights laws, a law against lynching, a federal fair employment practices committee, an end to Jim Crow (that is, to segregation) in interstate transportation, and protection of the right to vote.

The president's espousal of black rights was more than a tactical effort to disconnect the blacks and northern liberals from Wallace. He was pursuing a policy toward black Americans that was an emotional matter for him. At a White House luncheon for the executive committee of the Democratic national committee shortly after he sent the message to Congress in February 1948, a committeewoman from Alabama, Mrs. Leonard Thomas, addressed him: "I want to take a message back to the South," she said. "Can I tell them you're not ramming miscegenation down our throats? That you're for all the people, not just the North?" The president read the Bill of Rights to Mrs. Thomas. Then he said, "I'm everybody's President. I take back nothing of what I propose and make no excuse for it." A White

House waiter became so excited listening to the argument that he knocked a cup of coffee out of the president's hands. In a private letter to an old friend, a one-time corporal of Battery C, 129th Field Artillery, who had advised the president as a Southerner to go easy on the civil rights issue, Truman stated the issue bluntly: "The main difficulty with the South is that they are living eighty years behind the times and the sooner they come out of it the better it will be for the country and for themselves." So long as he remained in office, Truman wrote, he would continue the fight for equality of opportunity for all human beings. "When the mob gangs can take four people out and shoot them in the back, and everybody in the country is acquainted with who did the shooting and nothing is done about it, that country is in a pretty bad fix from a law enforcement standpoint. When a mayor and a city marshal can take a negro sergeant off a bus in South Carolina, beat him up and put out one of his eyes, and nothing is done about it by the state authorities, something is radically wrong with the system." When the Louisiana and Arkansas Railway continued to use black firemen after it converted from coal to oil, "it became customary for people to take shots at the negro firemen and a number were murdered" because such a white-collar job should go to a white man. "I can't approve of such goings on and . . . I am going to try to remedy it and if that ends up in my failure to be elected, that failure will be in a good cause."

The 1948 Democratic convention turned into a donnybrook over civil rights. Northern liberals, led by Hubert H. Humphrey, the young mayor of Minneapolis, who was soon to be elected to the Senate, were pushing for a commitment. The president hoped for a compromise that somehow could keep the southerners in the fold, although he admired the convention speeches of two black delegates and emotionally was on their side. But fifty-two southern congressmen had announced they would not support him in the November election, and they threatened to bolt the convention if it declared for civil rights. At that juncture, the northern liberals, supported by the big-city bosses, who cynically expected Truman to lose in November, sought black support for local candidates; the convention adopted the civil rights plank over southern protests.

The result was another body blow to Truman's election. The entire Mississippi delegation and half the Alabama delegation walked out of the convention; the other southern delegates remained but merely sat there without showing the slightest enthusiasm. Not long afterward, the southerners organized a party around the governor of South Carolina, J. Strom Thurmond. This Dixiecrat party obviously hoped to be spoilers in the election of 1948 and to force the Democratic party back to its old antiblack principles. A reporter asked Thurmond, who was no fool, why he was taking this extreme step. "President Truman is only following the platform that Roosevelt advocated," the reporter argued. "I agree," Thurmond said. "But Truman means it."

Omens for the campaign were poor, with a party split into left and right and with the Eisenhower support movement having barely collapsed. The president nonetheless took the nomination at 1:45 A.M., Thursday, July 15, with the fighting announcement: "Senator Barkley [his running mate] and I will win this election and make those Republicans like it—don't you forget that!" His impromptu speech stirred the convention. In the course of it, he announced a special session of Congress, called for July 26 (Turnip Day in Missouri—"turnips should be sown on the 26th of July wet or dry"), so that the Republican Eightieth Congress could enact all the measures it had been talking about throughout the spring and especially during the GOP convention, which had just ended. The speech brought cheers, and the campaign was on.

The omens for Truman's campaign were still poor. When he entered the convention hall to make his acceptance speech, the convention managers released fifty doves beneath a flowered liberty bell as a symbol of peace. Weak from the heat and hours of confinement, the birds were a sorry sight. One crashed into the balcony and flopped dead to the floor. "A dead pigeon," said one delegate, looking at Truman. The president refused to give up his high spirits, however, and laughed when a dove circled down toward the baldheaded chairman of the convention, House Minority Leader Rayburn. "One perched on Sam Rayburn's head," Truman recalled later. "Was Sam disgusted. Funniest thing in the convention."

The convention delegates did not really understand the fighting nature of their candidate. Truman went to the people, setting out on long trips by train to the far corners of the country to talk to between twelve and fifteen million voters in all. He lashed out at his opponents and talked about inflation, the Taft-Hartley Act, and civil rights. He took a decisive personal stand on each issue. When he mentioned farm aid, a Democratic principle going back to 1933, farmers began to wonder what the Republican party might do to their subsidies. He derided the Republican candidate, Governor Dewey, "whose name rhymes with hooey," and, of course, he harshly criticized the Eightieth Congress. "If you send another Republican Congress to Washington, you're a bigger bunch of suckers than I think you are!" he yelled. "Give 'em hell, Harry! Pour it on!" they yelled back.

The president contemptuously described the Congress that contained six more Republicans than Democrats in the Senate, fifty-seven more in the House, pointing out that they had had an opportunity to enact anything they wanted—an opportunity they had promptly muffed after Turnip Day. An easy target for Truman was Senator Taft, known as "Mr. Republican," who had told his fellow Americans during the meat shortage to eat less. Taft had long engaged Truman's ire because of his unctuousness and his unbending conservatism. It was said that, when the president flew in his presidential plane from Washington to Independence, he waited until the plane was over Taft's native Ohio before going to the bathroom. That was the way he felt about Taft, and the message got through to the senator. Referring to Truman's speeches from the back of the railroad car to smalltown gatherings, Taft told the Union League Club of Philadelphia that it was sad to see the American president "blackguarding Congress at every whistle station in the West." The Democratic national committee's publicity man, an imaginative man named Jack Redding, wired the mayors of thirty-five towns and cities through which the president's train had passed, asking if they agreed with Taft's description of their communities as whistlestops. "Must have the wrong city," responded the mayor of Eugene, Oregon. "Characteristically, Senator Taft is confused," wired the president of the Laramie, Wyoming, chamber of commerce. "Very poor taste," said the mayor of Gary, Indiana.

The president spoke to the people from morning to night, often getting up at 4:30 or 5:00 A.M., long before Mrs. Truman and Margaret were up, to talk with local politicians who got on at one stop and off at the next. Occasionally, he had a chance to look over the more formal speeches his assistants put together, checking out the description of villages and towns through which the train passed, so that, when he spoke off the cuff from the back of the railroad car, he could preface his remarks with commentaries about local places or people. Campaigning was an exhausting business—dawn to dusk, day after day, week after week. The president's throat burned, and his physician, Dr. Wallace Graham, prescribed a spray that anesthetized it and made speeches possible. There was always a possibility that a newspaperman would catch the president in a false statement; in his incessant talking, the president had to watch his instinct to say too much, and he had to keep his temper under control if something went wrong.

Truman's campaign train wound across the United States and back, snaking through a 31,700-mile trip, the most exhaustive by any president. This sort of campaign trip became unnecessary once nearly everyone had a television set in his living room, but that was after 1950—too late for Truman. In 1948, the president gave speeches in the old-fashioned way: an estimated 275 prepared speeches and, as Truman put it, "about 200 more off the record." The touring had begun even before the Phila-delphia convention, when advisers had arranged a long "non-

political" trip out West for the president on his way to receive an
honorary degree at the University of California at Berkeley. He
had used that tour to test the waters. The result had given him
confidence, although there were some bad moments, as when
his advance men failed to fill a huge hall in Omaha, and
photographers had a field day showing thousands of empty seats
with a fringe of listeners up front and the president of the United
States at the rostrum. At Carey, Idaho, he dedicated an airport
named for a young girl who had been killed in a private plane
crash to "the brave boy who died fighting for his country." The
nonpolitical tour had cost the Democratic national committee
nothing. Later tours had to be financed, however, and that was a
problem, for the campaign chest was empty. No one wanted to
pay a candidate's expenses when he was going to lose—as many
people thought, including the old financier and self-styled
adviser to presidents, Bernard Baruch, who tactlessly declined
an invitation to join the Democratic finance committee. Not
until September 14 was the president able to find a finance
chairman, Louis A. Johnson, who barely managed to raise the
money to take the train from one station to the next. In
Oklahoma City, there was not enough money to get the train out
of the station until local supporters passed the hat. Radio
stations cut the president off in midsentence for lack of money.
After a while Johnson turned this problem to advantage by
arranging to have them cut the president off, drawing attention
to the Democrats' shortage of campaign funds.

The contest seemed very uneven. The Republicans were
confident; their candidate did not refer to his opponent by
name, and he confined himself to platitudes so as not to lose
votes. His lackluster speeches were masterpieces of triteness.
"Our streams should abound with fish," he said, adding that he
would "cooperate with the farmer to protect all the people from
the tragedy of another dust bowl."

The Democratic candidate showed ever more strength, however. Truman spoke to integrated audiences in the American
South; at Rebel Stadium in Dallas, blacks sat with whites, for the

president refused to have it any other way. At Waco, when he shook hands with a black woman, the crowd booed, and the president boldly told them that black citizens have the same rights as whites. Frank J. Lausche, gubernatorial candidate in Ohio, gingerly got on the campaign train a few miles out of Dayton, and, fearful of associating with a loser, said he was getting off in the city. At the first stop en route, however, 7,000 persons roared their approval of Harry S. Truman, and Lausche's eyes opened wide. At Dayton, people were standing on each other in the station, and the massive crowd stretched out in every direction. "Is this the way all the crowds have been?" the governor asked cautiously. "Yes," said the president, "but this is smaller than we had in most states." "Well," said Lausche, "this is the biggest crowd I ever saw in Ohio." When the train moved out of Dayton on the way to Akron, Lausche was still aboard. It was the same everywhere. John Hersey, who wrote a profile of Truman for the *New Yorker* two years later, took his sons down to the railroad station in Connecticut to see the president go by and went home convinced that this man would be hard to beat. Under the brass there was steel; as Hersey put it, under "the exuberant, cocky joshing was a deep, unfeignable concern for these very people who crowded the tracks."

On the evening of election day, the results began to come in; Truman's votes mounted and those of Dewey crept up much more slowly, giving the president a plurality of 24,105,812 to Dewey's 21,970,065. The Wallaceites did some damage in New York, where they threw the state's huge electoral vote to Dewey, but Truman won unexpectedly in such rock-ribbed Republican states as Ohio, and he took California.

The nature of Truman's mandate in 1948—the authority granted him by the people—might well have seemed personal. It appeared that he had made it into a full term as president because of sheer grit, yet this appraisal, however flattering to Truman, is probably wrong. He won because of his very real personal qualities, of course; had he not possessed them, the electorate would have turned him out, as it many times has rid itself of unattractive figures. Still, the election was an affirmation of Roosevelt's New Deal, plus whatever additions Truman had brought to it. It was a maintaining election within the context of the New Deal tradition. Truman deserved great credit for succeeding in make a personal connection with the FDR tradition, notwithstanding all the harassment from the Dixiecrats and the Wallaceites, the right and the left. For all the whistle-stopping, however, 1948 was a low-turnout election, in which the Roosevelt Democratic coalition prevailed. Truman trailed the party ticket in key states. It also should be argued that, initial impressions to the contrary, the splits to left and right in the Democratic party may have helped Truman occupy the center of the spectrum. Dixiecrat opposition and the obvious waste of a vote for Wallace brought support for Truman from those who stressed civil rights; Wallaceite opposition deflected some of the redbaiting that otherwise would have assailed the Democrats.

The president's mandate, though personal, in a larger sense was support for the New Deal. He was not a man to linger over personal triumph, and he was keen for New Deal measures, so he took his mandate for what it was. No longer in the shadow of Roosevelt as a person, Truman was inaugurated in January 1949, with the help of an enormous appropriation voted by the Eightieth Congress when they assumed it would be for President Dewey, and he moved ahead with his own extension of Roosevelt's programs. He had set out his concerns more than three years before, in September 1945, in a huge, 16,000-word, twenty-one-point program. Among his proposals at that time were full employment and fair employment practices bills, federal control of the unemployment compensation program, a large housing program, and development of natural resources. His program of 1949 had twenty-four points and began with the following words: "Every segment of our population and every individual has the right to expect from our government a fair deal." The Fair Deal proposed control of prices, credit, commodities, exports, wages, and rents; a broadening of civil rights laws; low-cost housing; a seventy-five-cent minimum wage;

repeal of the Taft-Hartley Act; compulsory health insurance; increased coverage for social security; and federal aid to education. It may have been too ambitious a program, perhaps constituting a manifesto rather than a program. The president managed to get part of the Fair Deal through the Eighty-first Congress, however, and the rest gave the country a blueprint for the next decades. When civil rights met resistance in Congress, a Truman executive order set up an interdepartmental committee to enforce compliance with nondiscriminatory rules in government contracts. By the end of 1951, that order covered a fifth of the nation's economy. During the Korean War, the integration of the armed forces, begun in 1948, reached completion, forced if not by public opinion then by the need to form fighting units in Korea.

In the glow of electoral success, Truman sought to rationalize the nation's farm-support program with a plan known for its advocacy by his extraordinarily able secretary of agriculture, Charles F. Brannan. Brannan was a long-time high official of the Department of Agriculture. In 1948, by Truman's appointment, he became the only farm expert to rise to the office of secretary from within the department. Ever since 1933, a crazy-quilt of fixed prices and foolish measurements had assisted all farmers but mostly helped the big ones. The American consumer picked up the check for the support program in higher prices. Higher prices undercut exports, and the consumer picked up that loss when farmers sold their excess to the government at support prices. The consumer also paid for storing the excess. Sometimes the government sold it when prices went above support levels, but usually it was given away, at home or abroad.

Brannan proposed to support all farm products, not just a few, and to translate support into units, such as ten bushels of corn. The plan entitled each farmer to price support for 1,800 units—no more—thus eliminating the advantage of the big farmer. This also prevented the big farmer from taking enormous government payments and buying up land, raising land values. The unit support plan was also intended to encourage efficiency: the more cheaply, and hence efficiently, a farmer could produce each unit, the more profit he could make from the support price. In addition, the Brannan plan proposed direct subsidies rather than the prevailing complex arrangement of government loans and purchase agreements, and the plan proposed marketing agreements, pledging farmers to produce no more than they agreed—or at least to market no more. The Republicans preferred to let prices fall; Brannan recognized that falling prices encouraged ruinous overproduction. But the idea of direct payments was too socialistic for the Republicans, and the National Farm Bureau lined up behind the big farmers, who wanted to continue receiving thousands of dollars in disguised subsidies.

The Korean War came along before the Brannan Plan could get through Congress (although it nearly made it), and the war raised farm prices somewhat, giving just enough temporary succor to farmers to make them believe that they could get along as they had been. Another stopgap program passed Congress, rather than the thorough going plan the farm problem required. Consumers did not understand the technical discussion and tended to believe that all was well—for the farmers were out there farming, and the grocery stores were full of food. The annual budget of the Department of Agriculture during the Brannan years was about one billion dollars. Later, in the Eisenhower era, when agricultural production got out of hand because of good weather, new fertilizers, more stopgap measures, and no Brannan Plan, the annual department budget rose to ten billion dollars.

Thus passed the initial years of the Truman administration, full of turmoil and confusion, with far less accomplished for the American people than an idealist might have hoped, but with admirable proposals to the nation offered in times of support or no support. The heartwarming victory of 1948 was a personal triumph for Truman, and even more an acknowledgment of the correctness of his domestic program. Then, in the subsequent months of 1949 and 1950, the Fair Deal lost momentum. It was up against a torpor that postponed most of its enactment—a sluggishness caused by the end of World War II and the difficulties of adjustment. Perhaps the American people also were thinking in the cyclical political way, with periods of breathtaking reform followed by feelings of tiredness and slowing down. Americans failed to understand how rapid industrialization and urbanization brought problems that the laissez-faire ideas of the distant past could not solve. It was a time for big government; Washington had to assume tasks that were not taken up locally or on the state level, where there seemed to be perennially weak bureaucracies.

Despite the Fair Deal's tribulations, however, one thing was clear: no political figure of the twentieth century, not even Franklin Roosevelt, who showed extraordinary hesitation when the political going got rough, proved as willing as Truman to stand up for what he believed.

With General MacArthur

VI

The Korean War

ON THE EVENING of June 24, 1950, President Truman was in Independence, enjoying the leisure of the small town, the quiet of his rambling Victorian house at the corner of Delaware and Truman Road (as enthusiastic local Democrats had renamed the street). The house at 219 North Delaware—built just after the Civil War by Bess Truman's grandfather, George P. Gates, who had made a modest fortune from "Queen of the Pantry Flour"—had big rooms and high ceilings and was cool in the summer; the president enjoyed sitting there in a big, wing-backed chair, reading books of biography or history and letting problems in Washington take care of themselves.

But this time Washington problems refused to go away. Dean Acheson called that evening to relate startling news from the Far East. Fighting had broken out between North Korea and South Korea. In full battle array, with tanks and planes, the northerners—135,000 strong—were crossing the thirty-eighth parallel. Russian-made T-34 tanks were rumbling down roads, and when they met resistance the infantry was coming up and working their way forward.

The origins of this trouble in Korea went back to the end of World War II, and more remotely to the late nineteenth century. In the years when the house in Independence built by Bess Truman's grandfather was almost brand-new, far away on the other side of the world the little nation of Korea was becoming an object of contention between China, Russia, and Japan. Then, after wars with China in 1894–1895 and with Russia in 1904–1905, the Japanese had taken over the "hermit kingdom," had ruled it without mercy for dissident Koreans, and had left only when the Japanese empire collapsed at the end of World War II.

When the war of 1941–1945 reached its sudden end on August 14 with Japan's surrender, the occupation of the peninsula of Korea was arranged with great haste. The United States had no troops in the vicinity and made an agreement with the Soviet Union to divide Korea at roughly its halfway point, the thirty-eighth parallel, with more people and less territory below, fewer people and more land above. American troops then took over in the south. Had this division not been arranged, Russian troops could and probably would have occupied all of Korea.

What happened during the five years from the beginning of the American and Russian occupations to the outbreak of the Korean War was the virtually formal delineation of the thirty-eighth parallel as the boundary between north and south—with Communist rule in the north and the Republic of Korea under United Nations auspices in the south. The manner in which politics in the south turned into the dictatorship of the old Korean expatriate Syngman Rhee displayed the difficulties of trying to occupy, with the best of intentions, a country about which the people and leaders of the United States knew little or nothing.

Forty years of Japanese rule had made political leaders in South Korea hard to find. A few patriots had gone abroad, others had been imprisoned or killed by the Japanese, and many had made their peace with the Japanese and had prospered economically. To be sure, the people of Korea enjoyed no knowledge of freedom, knew nothing about politics, and did what the Japanese told them. The American occupation was initiated under the leadership of Lieutenant General John R. Hodge, an able corps commander who brought his troops into the penninsula shortly after the end of the war, only to see most of them "rotate" home and to find himself military governor of a place about which he knew very little. Its politics, Hodge soon learned, were distinctly different from those of his native Illinois. Hodge was a straight-thinking military man of good judgment, but he could not penetrate the Koreans' political factionalism; when this factionalism turned into riots, he wanted someone in Seoul who could ensure order. When President Truman thought about Korea, which was almost never, his outlook was much like that of Hodge.

Into this confused political world of Korean grays and American black-and-whites came Rhee, who had been abroad forty years, spoke fluent English, knew exactly what he wanted to do in Korea (attack the north and unify the country), and had the steely resolution to imprison his opponents and play up to the Americans. As soon as he took over as president of South Korea, the Americans became so fearful that he would attack the north that they denied his military forces any planes or tanks.

What brought on the Korean War was the opportunity Rhee's regime presented to the North Koreans. The United Nations had supervised an election in South Korea in 1948, with no cooperation from the North Koreans, and had certified South Korea as the Republic of Korea, an independent nation. American troops left the following year, except for a small group that remained to train the South Korean forces. The North Koreans then obtained the support of the Chinese or the Russians, or both, apparently planning to attack in the late summer of 1950; they moved up their timetable because the task seemed so easy.

When word came of the attack across the thirty-eighth parallel, Secretary Acheson saw no immediate need for the president to return to Washington. But when he called the next morning, Sunday, June 25, everything had turned deadly serious. South Korean resistance was crumbling, and Seoul, close to the border, was in danger. The president ordered his plane at the Kansas City airport and flew out so rapidly that he left several members of his staff behind.

When the presidential plane arrived in Washington, Truman went directly to Blair House, his residence during a major remodeling of the White House. That Sunday night, his principal advisers gathered for dinner and then sat around the dining table and agreed that the United States should resist the North Koreans. On the recommendation of General Douglas Mac-

Arthur, the Far Eastern commander, the president authorized the introduction of American air and naval forces on Tuesday, June 27, followed by commitment of ground forces June 30.

The decisions were those of the president, backed by his advisers and by the United Nations, where a resolution of support passed on the fourth day of fighting, June 27—the day American air and naval forces went in. The Security Council voted in favor of military measures, advising military support by all United Nations members. There was no Russian veto, because the Soviet delegate was not present. He had been boycotting Security Council meetings since the council had failed to seat Red China instead of Nationalist China in the permanent seat reserved for a Chinese delegate. Presumably, the Soviet delegate could not get instructions quickly enough to resume his seat and veto the resolution favoring intervention in Korea.

The Truman administration intervened in Korea for several reasons, one being that the Communist Chinese might be behind the attack. Americans had taken an interest in China for many years. In the year after the American Revolution, the first trading vessel had gone out to Canton, and hope for a huge China trade had flourished throughout the nineteenth and well into the twentieth century; unfortunately, that hope had never become a reality. Meanwhile, American missionaries had gone to China to civilize and Christianize the Chinese. Politically, there had been little American policy toward China, other than the championing of a commercial open door policy, which had been announced formally by Secretary of State John Hay at the end of the nineteenth century; the purpose of the open door policy was to prevent other commercially minded great powers from carving out territorial preserves so as to protect their own commerce and keep out competitors. Then, through a series of vicissitudes in the early twentieth century, the Chinese and Japanese had come into increasing conflict, as the Japanese confronted increasing Chinese nationalism. In 1931–1933 the

Japanese had taken Manchuria. Beginning in 1937, they had tried to take all of China, but the United States had objected, and the attack on Pearl Harbor resulted. World War II appeared to ensure Chinese freedom. At war's end, the regime of Generalissimo Chiang Kai-shek proved too weak to survive, however, and late in 1949 China passed under Communist control. During the mission of General Marshall in 1946, a combined Nationalist-Communist regime had seemed possible at first, but civil war had continued, and the Truman administration had sat back and waited for the dust to settle, which it did in 1949. Meanwhile, Democrats and Republicans had quarreled over what to do about China. There was no bipartisan approach to the Far East in the way that the Truman Doctrine, the Marshall Plan, the NATO alliance, and the Berlin airlift had all expressed bipartisan intentions for Europe. Truman's appointment of MacArthur to head up Japan's occupation in 1945 had removed that country from partisanship because of the general's well-known Republican leanings, but China had remained a political quandary. Both Democrats and Republicans were willing to give the Chinese $400 million in economic and military aid under the Marshall Plan, but neither party wanted to send U.S. Army divisions to China during the Chinese civil war. It was embarrassing to watch the Nationalist Chinese troops of Generalissimo Chiang Kai-shek lose battle after battle to the Communists because of bad morale and the poor leadership of Chiang. When General Albert C. Wedemeyer had gone to China on an investigative mission in 1947, Truman had suppressed his report because it would have "pulled the rug out from under" the Chinese Nationalist government; but, as Clark Clifford told the president, the Nationalists pulled it out from under themselves. When the Communists triumphed in 1949, neither the Truman administration nor the Republicans knew what to do. Suddenly, however, in June 1950, they came together in agreement on one possibility—that the Chinese Communists might have pushed the North Korean Communists into attacking South Korea. It was possible that Chinese Communist hatred of the United States lay at the bottom of the Korean attack. The Communist regime of Mao Tse-tung had talked of American imperial behavior. When the North Koreans attacked over the thirty-eighth parallel with Russian-supplied tanks and planes against the inadequately armed South Koreans, it seemed clear that the North Koreans were not acting for themselves and that Russian supplies had gone to them with at least the tacit support of the Chinese. The Chinese challenge became open when Communist Chinese forces entered the war in November 1950.

Admittedly, an alternative to the foregoing explanation was that the Soviet Union had encouraged the Chinese Communists to support the North Koreans in order to maintain leverage on the independent-minded group that had just organized a government in Peking. Perhaps even in 1949–1950 the Russians were uneasy about the victory of the Chinese Communists, fearful that the Chicoms, as the American military came to call the mainland Chinese, would be far more nationalist than communist and might prove to be embarrassing neighbors. Racial enmities between the Chinese and the Russians reached back for generations. When Stalin, in a burst of enthusiasm, had told the Japanese envoy Yosuke Matsuoka in the Moscow railway station in early 1941, "After all, we are both Asiatics," the remark had had a momentary purpose (buttering up the Russo-Japanese nonaggression pact, keeping the Japanese out of Siberia in case the Germans attacked in the west), but it was far from the truth about Russian feelings for Asiatics. The Russian empire had expanded into Asia in the eighteenth and nineteenth centuries, and the continuing problem of that expansion was the vast and perhaps unassimilable numbers of Asiatic peoples being brought into the Russian empire. The Soviet regime faced the same difficulty, and all the talk about autonomous Soviet republics was window-dressing. There was great danger that a strong Chinese regime in Peking, under whatever auspices, would attract the Asiatic citizens of Soviet Russia. There was every reason for the Soviets in 1949–1950 to regret the establishment of Communist China, out of fear that the new government would turn imperialistic and seek to rearrange the borders of the USSR. The theory that was heard at the time—that during the Korean War the Russians may have been trying to tie down the Chicoms in a conflict in Korea by supporting the North Koreans—may have had its basis in truth.

The position of the Soviet Union in regard to the Korean attack was difficult to calculate. Moscow may have been trying to tie down the Chinese Communists, but the Truman administration tended to believe that Moscow's purpose was something else: that the Soviets had allowed the North Korean attack as a feint to draw American forces to a remote Asian peninsula, after which the real attack would come in Western Europe against NATO, which was just being organized. The Cold War assuredly had been heating up. The Berlin blockade had ended in the summer of 1949, but in September the White House announced that the Soviet Union had exploded a nuclear device at the end of August. Added to that bad news was the announcement by the president in January 1950 that the United States was going ahead with development of an H-bomb.

Militarily, doing nothing about the Korean War would have had a catastrophic effect on the Japanese occupation, allowing the North Korean Communists to hold airfields within a short distance of Japan's major cities. The attack in Korea came near the only place in the Far East where the United States had substantial military forces, and not using those forces would raise many questions.

With the sudden news that the North Koreans had attacked and were moving almost unopposed into South Korea, the president revealed his feelings impulsively to Secretary of State Acheson, Undersecretary of State James E. Webb, and Secretary of Defense Johnson while driving from the airport to Blair House just before the conference on Sunday evening, June 25. He said that he did not think the Russians could support the action in Korea because of the limitations of the Trans-Siberian

Railroad and that this was a challenge the Americans had to meet. A quarter century later, Webb recalled that his words were something like "By God, I'm going to let them have it!" Johnson, sitting in a jump seat of the limousine, turned to face the president, put out his hand, and said, "I'm with you, Mr. President." It was an awkward moment, because of the personal rivalry that had developed between Johnson and Acheson; Johnson had been talking to newspapermen about Acheson and otherwise conspiring against him. Partly because of Johnson's behavior toward Acheson, the president a few months later forced the secretary of defense to resign. In the limousine, therefore, Webb thought he had better enter the conversation.

"Mr. President," he said, "we have done a great deal of work with all concerned during the last two days. We have distilled our recommendations into three specific ones, and I think you should hear these carefully worked out recommendations before making up your mind as to any action to be taken."

"Well, O.K., of course," the president in effect replied, "but you know how I feel."

Shortly afterward, Webb had an opportunity to say even more. The problem at that moment, just before the Blair House conference, was that Acheson and Webb wanted to put the Korean issue before the United Nations, so that any military action would be on an international basis. In a much-remarked speech the preceding January, Acheson had excluded Korea from the list of countries to which the United States had made a unilateral defense commitment. The secretary's enemies said afterward that he had given Korea to the Communists in that single speech. He had not, however, excluded Korea from those countries or areas whose defense was a multilateral concern. Acheson believed that American military action had to follow rather than precede international support. The president seemed to want action immediately, however, and Johnson was supporting him. When the president's car reached Blair House, Johnson and Acheson entered the house and turned to the left into a room filled with officials, while Truman turned to the

the right, into another cloakroom. Webb walked in after him, closed the door, and outlined the three military steps that he and Acheson thought necessary: the use of first the air force, second the navy, and third the ground forces, with the third step coming after a day or two—because the Security Council was meeting in New York. Truman and Webb then left the cloak-room together and walked to the meeting.

At the beginning, the Korean War was touch and go. The administration had not intended a stand, and therefore nothing was ready. Night and day, from the cumbersome bureaucracy of the Pentagon in Washington, the clattering teletypes sent in-structions to MacArthur's bureaucracy in the Dai Ichi building in Tokyo. A sense of deep crisis filled both cities. The northerners, with their tanks and planes, moved relentlessly south, while the South Korean army faded away.

The first U.S. Army contingent was a hastily organized force consisting of two companies of Charles B. (Brad) Smith's 1st Battalion, 21st Infantry, reinforced by a platoon of recoilless antitank rifles and 4.2 inch mortars, totaling 406 officers and men. It was limited in size by the number of available C-54 planes to fly it to Korea from Itazuke, the U.S. Air Force base nearest Korea. After landing near Pusan, Smith's battalion put up a good fight but was unable to stop the advance; the enemy armor and accompanying infantry, which outnumbered the Americans almost 300 to 1, was able to outflank Smith's successive positions.

Meanwhile the garrison in Japan threw off the torpor of years of routine garrison duty, girlfriends and ice cream and candy bars and movies. The occupying forces in Japan were shifted to Korea as fast as transport planes and ships could take them, in the hope of saving Pusan, the port at the southeastern tip of the peninsula.

What a change it was for the Japan garrison! General Matthew B. Ridgway afterward recalled the smell of Korea, forever fixed in his mind as once it had fixed itself in his nostrils—the smell of excrement, of putridity beyond measure. Generations of hard work and survival were manifested in the smell, which Ridgway said was epitomized by the Korean sauce known as Kim-Chi. From the great crock that every Korean peasant kept next to his kitchen stove, filled with overripe cabbage, fishheads, and entrails, was drawn a brown-black fluid that sent G.I.s retching outdoors. The soft-living American garrison from Japan descended into this primitive economy and moved up from Pusan toward the approaching North Koreans; they encountered hardened enemies who never had known ice cream and who had trained under veterans of World War II who had been Korean volunteers in the Soviet army. Adept at infiltration, unaccustomed to jeeps and trucks, unburdened with gear, the North Koreans came at the Americans in an unequal contest. The Americans clogged the narrow roads with vehicles, and the North Koreans moved around them along the ridges. Occasionally, the American convoys were shot up like cornered rats.

Gradually getting fresh troops over to Korea and off the roads into the fields and hills, the American commanders brought order around Pusan. By early August they had established a line and held it with artillery, and MacArthur in Tokyo and the administration in faraway Washington breathed easier. It was not long, however, before Major General William F. Dean of the 24th Division, who was trying to defend a burning town with a few men, running from building to building carrying a bazooka and finally trapped in a ditch, was taken prisoner. All of South Korea was lost, down to a line around Pusan, but the port held, and the teletypes—Washington to Tokyo and also to London, Paris, Frankfurt, and Rome—still clattered.

The president sent out the chief of naval operations, Admiral Forrest P. Sherman, and the army's able chief of staff, General J. Lawton (Lightning Joe) Collins. They checked out the Pusan perimeter and talked to MacArthur, who insisted on an amphibious attack against Inchon, midway up on Korea's west side near Seoul. Neither the navy nor the army brass much liked the idea, but they went along with it. The attack was a complete success. The troops made their way at high tide in a treacherous channel which twisted through mile-wide mud flats. They reached the beach without opposition and rapidly moved inland before the tide turned and stranded the ships. MacArthur sent the Inchon force, the X Corps, eastward into the peninsula. Shortly afterward, the besieged Eighth Army to the south, at Pusan, moved north to catch the overextended North Koreans in a pincer. Within days of the Inchon operation on September 15, 1950, the North Koreans caved in, and on September 29 the U.S. Army completed the recapture of Seoul.

Retaking the South Korean capital emboldened everyone— MacArthur, the joint chiefs, Secretary Acheson, President Truman, and America's allies in the United Nations. This led to a horrendous miscalculation: the decision to send United Nations troops north of the thirty-eighth parallel. No one stopped to consider that such a move meant destroying a Communist government. Nothing like it had been done before. The end of World War II had divided Germany and Austria and had separated Eastern Europe from Western Europe, and leaders of the United States and the Soviet Union recognized these divisions. In the Far East, however, the Western nations seemed to think the dividing line in Korea was impermanent. The Truman administration authorized MacArthur to cross the parallel on September 27, and the United Nations General Assembly supported the move on October 7. Washington advised MacArthur to limit the advance troops to those of the reconstituted South Korean divisions then fighting with the Americans. MacArthur ignored that part of his instructions, and flung his troops, including the Americans, headlong into the north toward the Yalu and Tumen rivers, Korea's boundary with Manchuria. By this time the X Corps was on the move: one division had been sent by rail to Pusan, the other loaded aboard ship at Inchon and brought around the peninsula. Both then moved northward by sea along the peninsula's east side to Wonsan, above the 38th parallel. The Eighth Army, now up from Pusan, moved along the western side. Command of the two forces, X Corps and Eighth Army, was independent; Lieutenant General Edward M.

Almond and Lieutenant General Walton H. Walker both reported to Tokyo.

The Chinese Communist regime in Peking protested the crossing of the parallel volubly and bitterly, through the agency of the Indian ambassador, K. M. Pannikar, a man whom many considered too friendly to the Chinese.

Truman sensed an uneasy situation in Korea and yet did not fully grasp its danger when he flew out to Wake Island in mid-October and met MacArthur for the first time. The general had claimed grandly that he was too busy with the war to come back to the United States, which he should have done, as he had not visited his own country since 1937. Truman took him at his word, and flew the enormous distance and back, 14,404 miles. The meeting went well enough, and MacArthur assured the president that, even if the Chinese Communists entered the conflict, the greatest number of troops they could hope to maintain in Korea was from 50,000 to 60,000. He said that the United Nations had won the war, and that it would be possible to send a division from Korea to Europe in January 1951. The two talked for an hour. According to Truman, MacArthur wore a "greasy ham and eggs cap that evidently had been in use for twenty years" and had his shirt unbuttoned, which was irritating to the president, but otherwise everything was very friendly, and Truman left with a much better feeling for the general. He flew to San Francisco, made a speech, and returned to Washington.

In retrospect, the Wake Island conference was a poor idea. There was no public policy reason for the president to go so far to meet a general, any general, and the talk had lasted only an hour. Perhaps the general was too much a Republican for him to be invited to Washington. The president's aides apparently told Truman: "If he comes here, everyone will want him to talk and the Republicans will have a field day using him to attack you." Senator William F. Knowland of California claimed that the president had gagged MacArthur on policy toward Chiang Kai-shek, then domiciled in Taiwan, and to ungag him in Washington might make a mess. The president's purpose in going to

Wake Island may have been something else, however. Truman
never confessed to another political purpose, but it did look as if
he was making a grandstand play before the 1950 congressional
elections, giving the impression that the war was under control
and that the time was right to reelect the Democratic Congress
and to elect any other Democrats running for office. This
purpose, if such it was, was no worse—and far less irresponsible—than President Franklin Roosevelt's decision to go along
with the British in 1942 and send American troops into North
Africa in what he hoped would be an attack before the congressional elections, on the principle that American troops had
to fight somewhere during the election year. The theatrical
aspect of the Wake Island meeting with the general wearing the
"ham and eggs cap" was nonetheless bothersome.

After Wake Island, the bottom almost dropped out of the
Korean War. MacArthur's assurance to the contrary, the Chinese
sent 300,000 men across the frozen Yalu and Tumen and
positioned them in the mountains. Early in November, they
sallied forth with a blast of bugles and shouting of obscenities,
with mortars and Russian Katusha rockets. They attacked
viciously for several days, inflicting hundreds of casualties,
and disappeared as quickly as they had come. On Sunday,
November 26, after American forces, unshielded by South
Korean troops, had reached the Yalu and gazed across its frozen
length to Manchuria, thirty-three divisions of Communist Chinese
launched a massive counteroffensive. American forces reeled; the
X Corps had to evacuate, and the Eighth Army retreated south of
Seoul. General Walker was killed in a jeep crash, and General
Ridgway replaced him. For a while it looked like catastrophe—
evacuation of the peninsula.

It was a time of sheer crisis. In Washington, the president
had the stouthearted support of the joint chiefs and Secretary
Acheson, and behind them stood a confused but resolute nation,
ready to do whatever was necessary to protect the country's
honor and that of the United Nations. The news from Korea was
grim, however; it resembled news a few years earlier in late 1944,

during the Battle of the Bulge, when each day the pins on the maps, division and brigade and regimental flags, moved back and the battle lines were erased and redrawn in uncertainty—winding, weaving, sagging. There were meetings every day, limousines drawing up in the alley behind Blair House or near the Oval Office in the west wing of the White House.

Meanwhile, on November 1, two young Puerto Rican nationalists, Griselio Torresola and Oscar Collazo, attempted to assassinate the president. They approached Blair House along the sidewalk, from different directions, and tried to bound up the steps. They exchanged fire with the guards, and Torresola was killed and Collazo wounded and captured. Two Blair House guards were also wounded, and Officer Leslie Coffelt was killed. The president put his head out the upstairs window to see what was going on and one of the guards shouted, "Get back!", which Truman gingerly did. For the rest of his time in office, the president knew he could be shot at any moment, although he told his cousin Ethel Noland he was unafraid, for experts had shot at him in 1918.

The president made a bad mistake in his press conference on November 30. He read a statement that was straightforward but not highly quotable, nothing that a hardboiled city-desk man would consider news, so when he ended his reading, the reporters proceeded to do some news manufacturing. Truman could be decisive to a fault at a press conference, and the reporters knew it. One of them asked about weapons the United States would use in Korea as a result of the Chinese intervention, and the president gave the impression that he would "let the Chinese have it." "Will that include the atomic bomb?" asked a reporter. "That includes every weapon we have," said the president flatly. This was reported in indirect discourse, but it certainly was reported. The British government under Prime Minister Clement Attlee had been increasingly unsure of MacArthur, fearing that Truman might not control him. Attlee did not trust Washington's judgment on nuclear weapons, so he immediately invited himself to Washington. Truman did not

desire the visit but could not refuse. He did his best to make
Attlee feel better, but he listened with horror to the Britisher's
willingness to wind up the Korean War through what the prime
minister described as "negotiation" with the Chinese and
Russians—a negotiation the Truman administration considered
nothing short of surrender.

Late one afternoon during the Attlee visit, Truman learned
that his high school chum of fifty years, Charlie Ross, had
collapsed and died at his desk in the west wing. That night the
president went to daughter Margaret's first formal Washington
concert at Constitution Hall. It was a tight, strained evening,
because he and Mrs. Truman did not tell Margaret of Charlie's
death before the concert. Early the next morning, already edgy,
the president read a savage review of Margaret's performance in
the *Washington Post* by the newspaper's music critic, Paul Hume.
"She is flat a good deal of the time," Hume wrote. "She cannot
sing with anything approaching professional finish. . . . She
communicates almost nothing of the music she presents."
Impulsively, Truman took a piece of White House stationery
from a drawer and wrote a longhand letter to Hume; he
reconsidered and wrote a revision. In the second draft, he said
Hume sounded like a "frustrated old man who never made a
success, an eight-ulcer man on a four-ulcer job, and all four
ulcers working," that he was lower than the columnist West-
brook Pegler, whom Truman detested, and that, if he could lay
his hands on Hume, the reviewer would need "a new nose and
plenty of beefsteak and perhaps a supporter below." It being
early, with no secretaries in the office, Truman took the letter
outside to a mailbox and dropped it in. The letter was quickly
published, making the president look silly. Margaret first said
her father could not have written it, then had to amend her
statement, and the president was more embarrassed. The year
1950 ended in this depressing manner.

Shortly afterward, the news from Korea turned around.
Ridgway skillfully saved the war on lines fifty miles south of the
thirty-eighth parallel, invigorating the men by his wonderful

presence right up at the front—chin up, eyes snapping, grenades hanging ostentatiously from regulation shoulder straps. After walking his lines, the doughty general brought in artillery, sited it against the stupidly immobile and bunched Chinese forces, and traversed their lines with withering fire, slaughtering thousands of men. The army called it Operation Killer. In a second offensive known as Operation Ripper, Ridgway's troops fought their way back to the thirty-eighth parallel and a skewed line slightly below the parallel on one side and on the other slightly above. This line held through the rest of that year and through the following year, until the truce in 1953.

Many times during the hectic weeks beginning in late November 1950, the president and his advisers must have thought ruefully of their decision to cross the parallel. How much better it might have been in September–October to have left well enough alone. But they had made the error, and thereafter the only course was to attempt to undo its consequences.

In addition to the massive error of crossing the parallel, we now can see that the president made two other misjudgments during the Korean War. At the outset, he failed to ask Congress for a declaration of war. He had asked Senator Tom Connally privately if he should, and Connally had said no: "If a burglar breaks into your house, you can shoot at him without going down to the police station and getting permission. You might run into a long debate by Congress, which would tie your hands completely. You have the right to do so as Commander in Chief and under the UN Charter." Truman took Connally's advice and formally described the war as a "police action." A declaration, however, would have registered overwhelming congressional approval and would have given the war legal sanction. The police action was easy for GOP partisans to challenge, especially during the years of truce negotiations. During the truce talks, the North Korean negotiators, backed by the Chinese, refused to bend on the issue of forced repatriation of tens of thousands of anticommunist North Korean prisoners. Many Republicans abandoned their enthusiasm for the police action and, so long as the murder and enslavement did not involve their countrymen, the repatriation issue seemed to them merely a technicality preventing the end of Mr. Truman's war—dishonored successor to Mr. Madison's war, Mr. Polk's, Mr. Lincoln's, Mr. McKinley's, Mr. Wilson's, and Mr. Roosevelt's. It is true, of course, that the Republicans probably would have attacked Truman whether or not there had been a declaration of war. When the war faltered, when the entry of the Chinese raised the prospect of a prolonged conflict, and certainly when the MacArthur issue clouded everything, the GOP partisans would have attacked. Still, in addition to all the other inviting reasons for jumping on the president of the United States, they had the fact of an undeclared war.

Truman's third error was a result of poor advice from the usually astute Speaker of the House, Sam Rayburn. The president wanted price controls, but Rayburn advised against them; remembering their wartime unpopularity, Truman assented. Prices shot up, however, and Congress did not give the president authority to freeze them until January 1951, by which time it was too late. The inflation during the first months of the Korean War thus encouraged its critics.

Not an error on Truman's part—indeed, an utterly necessary action, although it poured oil on the flames of the war's increasing unpopularity—was his firing of General MacArthur in April 1951. The president was defending the Constitution. Admittedly, there were personal feelings involved; Truman had disliked MacArthur ever since 1942, when the general had gone to Australia instead of remaining in the Philippines and surrendering with his men, and had accepted a congressional medal of honor for himself while denying one for Lieutenant General Jonathan M. Wainwright, who had stayed behind. (In 1979, it was revealed that, in early 1942, MacArthur had accepted a tax-free gift of $500,000 from President Manuel Quezon of the Philippines, in appreciation for his services, just before he had arranged for Quezon to leave the islands by submarine.) "I'm not very fond of MacArthur," Senator Truman had written to his daughter in 1942. "If he'd been a real hero he'd have gone down with the ship." He wrote again in 1944: "No good soldier is a speechmaker or a showman. That's why we don't like Dugout Douglas from Australia." After his meeting with the general at Wake Island in 1950, the president had a much more favorable view of MacArthur and said that "Mac" was a good and loyal soldier; but the Far Eastern commander himself disdained Truman, whom he later described to a newspaperman as "the little bastard." MacArthur believed that, as commander in the Far East, he knew better how to beat the Chinese—better than did the secretary of defense, General Marshall, who replaced Johnson in September 1950 and had been a colonel in 1935 when MacArthur was chief of staff, and better than did the joint chiefs of staff.

The Korean War tarnished the general's military reputation, for he made egregious tactical errors. John Foster Dulles, in Tokyo on June 25, 1950, fresh from a visit to Korea, went to MacArthur's apartment and heard him say that "this is just a border foray, and those tanks will soon run out of gas, and the whole thing will be over." It was an incredible appraisal, showing the general's willingness to play hunches, right or wrong. After weeks of difficulty, when the line held at Pusan and the general arranged the attack on Inchon, success emboldened him. At Wake Island he assured the president that the Chinese would not intervene, but when they did he lost his nerve and advised Washington to withdraw. "We face an entirely new war," he announced on November 28, 1950; " . . . this command . . . is now faced with conditions beyond its control and strength."

An intolerable situation arose when MacArthur interfered three times in the war's grand strategy. In August 1950, he sent a statement to the annual encampment of the Veterans of Foreign Wars and Truman read an advance copy; the statement advocated making Formosa a United States bastion. An instruction from the president forced MacArthur to withdraw the statement, although it already had been published. Then, in December

1950, the general told *US News and World Report* that "extraordinary inhibitions . . . without precedent in military history" denied him the opportunity to carry the war into the privileged sanctuary of the enemy, Communist China. In response, a directive from the president, dated December 6, forbade any speech, press release, or public statement without clearance. On March 20, 1951, the joint chiefs informed MacArthur that the State Department was planning a presidential announcement that the United Nations was preparing to discuss conditions of a settlement in Korea. Four days later, on his own and with no warning, MacArthur offered to negotiate and, in his usual florid style, threatened the Chinese with destruction of their homeland: "The enemy, therefore, must by now be painfully aware that a decision of the United Nations to depart from its tolerant effort to confine the war to the area of Korea, through an expansion of our military operations to his coastal areas and interior bases, would doom Red China to the risk of imminent military collapse." Shortly afterward, MacArthur sent a letter to the Republican minority leader, Representative Joe Martin of Massachusetts, again setting out his ideas. On April 5, 1951, Martin read the letter to the House. "It seems strangely difficult for some to realize," the general wrote, "that here in Asia is where the Communist conspirators have elected to make their play for global conquest, and that we have joined the issue thus raised on the battlefield; that here we fight Europe's war with arms while the diplomats there still fight it with words; that if we lose the war to Communism in Asia the fall of Europe is inevitable, win it and Europe most probably would avoid war and yet preserve freedom. As you point out, we must win. There is no substitute for victory."

MacArthur had become an impossible proconsul. The United Nations allies, especially the British, were fearful of his rash moves and pressed the administration to control him. Because the Constitution's provision for supremacy of the political over the military was clearly in the balance, Truman removed him.

There was great public uproar when the general came back to

the United States. His plane touched down first in San Francisco, where a crowd estimated at 100,000 greeted him at City Hall. MacArthur went on to the East Coast, where, in sepulchral tones, he addressed a joint session of Congress, ending his speech with a line from an old barrack ballad: "Old soldiers never die, they just fade away."

In New York City the general did anything but fade; MacArthur Day festivities were tumultuous. The department of sanitation reported that the MacArthur parade litter weighed 16.6 million pounds; the previous record had been 3.6 million from a parade for Charles A. Lindbergh in 1927. Great receptions followed in other cities as well.

Congress rushed to investigate the general's removal, and hearings began before the combined Senate foreign relations and military affairs committees. Gradually, however, the hearings displayed MacArthur's impulsiveness, the uncertainty of his appraisals, his monomania about the Far East as compared to Europe. In this latter respect, the chairman of the joint chiefs of staff, General Omar N. Bradley, put the Truman administration's reasoning succinctly. "Taking on Red China," Bradley said at the hearings, would have led only "to a larger deadlock at greater expense. . . . So long as we regarded the Soviet Union as the main antagonist and Western Europe as the main prize," the strategy advanced by MacArthur "would involve us in the wrong war at the wrong place at the wrong time and with the wrong enemy."

All this said nothing about MacArthur's refusal to follow orders. President Truman had insisted on the right of the nation's chief executive to establish foreign policy and military strategy, and MacArthur had directly challenged the president. A majority of Americans probably believed MacArthur was right, the president wrong. People later came to see their error, but at the time Truman aroused irrational feelings in millions of his countrymen. "That must have taken a bit of courage," said a reporter to Truman, years after the event. "Courage had nothing to do with it," snapped the retired president, his eyes flashing. "He was insubordinate and I fired him."

By the end of the Truman administration in January 1953, the Korean War was still on; it did not come to an armistice until July 27. The war cost 33,629 American battle deaths and as many as two million Korean and Chinese lives, both military and noncombatant. It was not a small conflict by historical standards.

Strangely, the armistice was achieved by a threat of the same military tactics that General MacArthur had urged upon Truman and that the president had steadfastly resisted. Late in May the new Eisenhower administration threatened the Chinese Communists with an extension of the war, including use of nuclear weapons, unless the negotiations at Panmunjom came to a close. The war stopped on this jarring note. One had the uneasy feeling that MacArthur in defeat was MacArthur triumphant. His public statements during 1950–1951 were impossible—not for a moment could Truman have tolerated his insubordination—but the succeeding Republican administration secured peace by threatening to employ his tactics.

There was another consequence of the hostilities in Korea, in this instance a long-term result, that Truman must have found as distasteful as the way the war halted: the militarization of American life that followed the Korean War. Before the war, the annual military budget was running in the neighborhood of $15 billion. After the war began, there was a good deal of criticism that the slow American response, throwing in such units as Task Force Smith, occurred because the budget was far too low—that Truman starved the military. It was true that in 1949 the president appointed the chairman of his 1948 campaign finance committee, Johnson, to replace the ailing Forrestal as secretary of defense, so that Johnson would cut the budget. (Shortly afterward, Forrestal committed suicide, realizing that he had unduly delayed unification of the armed forces.) Johnson was a suitably blunt instrument to force the three squabbling military services—army, navy, and air force—into a tight budget, and Truman approved his course.

The president had never fully trusted regular officers, having dealt with them during World War I; he believed the country's best defense lay in the National Guard. Early in 1950, a top-secret National Security Council report known as NSC-68 advised tripling the military budget; the administration had been considering this recommendation desultorily when the Korean War opened. Years later, in 1975, NSC-68 was declassified and published; it proved to be an unimpressive document, full of rhetorical anticommunism. The Truman administration had known this; in 1950 one of Truman's White House assistants, probably George Elsey, a Harvard-trained historian, had annotated a copy of NSC-68 that is now in the Truman Library, pointing out its exaggerations—what afterward became known as Cold War rhetoric. When the Korean War began, however, it had been necessary to increase the military budget dramatically—as it turned out, by a factor of three. This had been the recommendation of NSC-68, and the document was thus adopted, whatever that meant, as national policy. After the war, the military budget never went down; during the 1950s, it continued to go up, though gradually. President Eisenhower's much-noted "farewell address" of 1961 warned against a military-industrial complex, the push of weapons technology that, in the 1950s, produced a virtual alliance between the military and weapons manufacturers. This situation was an awkward heritage of the Korean War.

In Truman's last years, troubled by illness, he was mercifully unable to observe the third haunting result of the Korean War—the waging of an undeclared war in Vietnam, with its attendant public tumult and eventually a national humiliation.

Abbie Rowe, National Park Service

With Adlai Stevenson

VII

Communism and Corruption

THE PRESIDENTIAL ELECTION of 1952 was fought on what Senator Karl E. Mundt of South Dakota, cochairman of the GOP speakers bureau, described as a winning formula: K^1C^2—Korea, communism, and corruption. The supposed chemistry of these horrors was unclear, but it was possible for the Republicans to give the appearance of science and conclude that, with an end to what Senator Nixon loosely described as twenty years of treason, everything would come into order, virtue would triumph, and the millennium would begin under a Republican administration.

Suspicion of conspiracy was at an all-time high in the late 1940s and early 1950s—higher than the anti-French agitation of the 1790s, higher than the red scare of the early 1920s. The almost blind hatred of communism at the time is difficult to comprehend in retrospect, although it traced back for decades into the American past. In the 1880s and 1890s, the socialist movement in Europe appeared in America, carried mostly by immigrants. It bothered many native Americans, who felt that it was distinctly a European idea, contrary to American tradition and confirmed by nothing in American experience. They believed that anyone who worked hard could get ahead and would never be held back by class prejudice or the economic system. European socialism had minor repercussions on the American scene, but anarchism—which seemed to be part of socialism—became a deadly serious issue because of the bloody Haymarket riot in Chicago in 1886 and the assassination of President McKinley by an anarchist in Buffalo in 1901.

The roots of the belief in conspiracy during the Truman era lay more in the twentieth century than the nineteenth, and developed from American concern for the course of revolution in Russia. During World War I, Americans celebrated the changeover of the Russian government from despotism to a republic in March 1917. Then, in November, came the Bolshevik revolution, which was surrounded by a sort of violence that was impossible to ignore. Frivolous comments by Bolshevik leaders such as Lenin, that it was necessary to break eggs to make an omelet, were contemptible excuses for the revolution's enormous human cost. Such excuses did not justify, either, the famine caused in the 1930s by the collectivization of agriculture and then the senseless purges of the army and bureaucracy and intelligentsia, which cost millions of lives.

The wartime collaboration of the United States with Soviet Russia was always a distant one—the two fronts connected tenuously by shipment of lend-lease through Iran. It was an awkward collaboration at best, and the American people never quite accepted it. When the war was over and Russian animus appeared, it was not difficult for Americans to remember the Soviet past and the socialist and anarchist ideas and actions of earlier years. By the late 1940s, everything was made to order for belief in communist conspiracy.

Three groups of onetime New Deal supporters were ready to believe that communism imperiled America and Americans: Midwesterners, relatively recent immigrants, and Catholics. Isolation, persecution abroad, and strong belief in the Church all produced enemies. Such groups were willing to believe the contentions of the American ambassador to China at the end of the war, the Oklahoma oilman Patrick J. Hurley, who had been secretary of war during the Hoover administration and a major general in the U.S. Army. Hurley said he had uncovered a nest of communist subversion in his own embassy in Chungking, where a group of subordinates who spoke Chinese and knew China (the ambassador failed on both counts) thought they knew better courses for China policy than he did and recommended, over his protest, that the United States aid the Communist Chinese as well as the Nationalists. His subordinates claimed that the Communists, unlike the Nationalists, fought the Japanese and that, unlike the Nationalists, their leaders were incorruptible and had much popular support. Hurley fumed and stormed over this recommendation from his staff and managed to disperse the dissidents far and wide in the foreign service, breaking up a group of trained observers of Chinese politics that was dearly needed in coming years, when China policy proved so difficult. One of the men he forced out, John Stewart Service, came back to Washington and became associated with Philip J. Jaffe, the coeditor of a New York magazine, *Amerasia*. In June 1945, the FBI arrested Service, Jaffe, and several others because the magazine had published a classified paper of the wartime intelligence organization, the Office of Strategic Services. The *Amerasia* office contained a cache of six hundred secret and top-secret documents, and the FBI believed that someone might have been photographing them for transmission to Moscow. Service was released because of lack of evidence against him. In addition, because the FBI had conducted illegal searches, the evidence against Jaffe and a State Department employee, Emmanuel Larsen, was not admissible in court, and these two principal defendants were let off with small fines. The affair added to the certainty of believers in conspiracy that something against the American national interest was afoot.

There was no uncertainty about the case of Igor Gouzenko, a code clerk in the Soviet embassy in Ottawa who defected in September 1945 and provided documents that showed a Russian espionage ring involving a British scientist, Allan Nunn May, in the wartime nuclear program. Canadian Prime Minister W. L. Mackenzie King telephoned Truman and came to Washington with the bad news, for much of the ring's operations had been within the United States. With the Gouzenko defection, the president knew for the first time that the Russians had penetrated the Manhattan Project and that Stalin's apparent indifference to Truman's announcement at Potsdam that the United States had perfected a new weapon of great explosive power was, in fact, feigned.

It took time to analyze the Gouzenko documents, which made obscure references to unidentified spies within the American government. In February 1946, however, the FBI obtained testimony from two admitted former Communists, Elizabeth T. Bentley and Whittaker Chambers, the latter a feature editor for *Time* magazine, implicating a senior official of the State Department, Alger Hiss, and an assistant secretary of the treasury, Harry Dexter White. Hiss was soon to become president of the Carnegie Endowment for International Peace, and Truman had nominated White as United States director of the International Monetary Fund. It was an awkward situation for Truman to deal with, considering that the accusations were unsubstantiated. The president consulted Chief Justice Fred M. Vinson and Attorney General Tom Clark and decided to let the FBI continue its investigation quietly. White died in 1948, two days after denying all accusations before the House Un-American Activities Committee, and his case lapsed. In August 1948, however, Chambers openly accused Hiss, who brought suit for libel, and two trials followed. The first trial resulted in a hung jury, but the jury in the second trial, in January 1950, convicted Hiss of perjury for saying that he never had passed classified State Department papers to Chambers and for denying that he had had contact with Chambers after 1937. The question of espionage, involving two batches of State Department documents for 1937–1938 that had come into Chambers's possession, was impossible to resolve because of the statute of limitations, a common law proviso that no court may try a citizen for espionage after a five-year lapse between the event and the indictment.

As a public issue, the Hiss case lingered for a generation and more, even to the present. In a press conference after Chambers testified against Hiss, Truman agreed that the affair was an excuse for the Republican party to keep from doing what it ought to do, which was to deal with serious problems of foreign and domestic policy rather than attacking innocent people. It was an unfortunate remark for Truman to have made, since Hiss later was convicted and went to jail. Also unfortunate were the supportive testimony of Justice Felix Frankfurter of the Supreme Court, who testified to Hiss's probity, and Secretary Acheson's press conference statement that he was not going to turn his back on Alger Hiss. The administration paid dearly for these comments in support of an apparent traitor.

The time from late January into early February 1950 was the worst time for the Truman administration, at least in respect to the communism issue. The second Hiss trial ended in conviction on January 21. To all appearances it had been a fair trial, conducted with decorum by an experienced federal judge, in contrast to the questionable procedures in the first trial. Hiss's conviction became a subject of several books, and readers argued the case, but for the majority of Americans the second trial established his guilt.

It was only ten days later that the administration announced its program to construct the superbomb. Then, on February 3, the British government revealed the confession of Dr. Klaus Fuchs, an eminent nuclear physicist and German refugee who had become a British subject, that he had passed to the Soviets the topmost secrets of the Anglo-American wartime and early postwar nuclear program. Fuchs had been present at Los Alamos and had passed everything he knew there to the Soviets. Later, he had made his contacts in London by various methods—such as going into a pub carrying a copy of the weekly paper *Tribune* and taking a seat on a certain bench (his contact would be carrying a red book), or going to a private house and throwing a periodical over the fence with a message inserted on the tenth page. In early 1949, he broke off his spying after reconsidering his actions of preceding years; he had given the information to the Russians because of his conviction that they loved peace as much as did the British and the Americans. The FBI and British intelligence were moving in his direction when, in a fit of remorse for having betrayed his friends at the British nuclear center of Harwell, and under extraordinarily skillful interrogation by a British intelligence officer, he confessed. His confession revealed that none of the bomb secrets had ever been secret.

His description of his confederates implicated two Americans, Harry Gold and David Greenglass, who were picked up in New York. They in turn implicated Julius and Ethel Rosenberg, who were tried for espionage, convicted, and executed in 1953. The Rosenberg trial created some uncertainty among newspaper readers because these two supposed master spies, whom the government claimed headed the ring involving Fuchs, did not look the part—they were unassuming people of ordinary appearance. Also, curiously, they never showed any willingness to admit to what the prosecution accused them of doing. They went to their deaths in the electric chair at Sing Sing, one after the other, without flinching. The case has remained a perplexing one, and the subject of great debate ever since.

All the while (and never sufficiently understood by Americans) a diabolically successful spy ring was operating in the British embassy in Washington. In the early 1930s, the ring's members—Guy Burgess, Donald Maclean, and Harold A. R. (Kim) Philby—had attended Cambridge University, where they had developed an interest in communism and had evidently been recruited as agents for the Soviets. During World War II, these three men rose in the British intelligence organization. After the war, Burgess and Maclean were in the embassy in Washington, where they had access to nuclear secrets. Philby also came to Washington, as liaison between British intelligence and the CIA. In 1948 the foreign office promoted Maclean to head of chancery of the embassy in Cairo, a Class A embassy that gave access to sensitive information. Then both Burgess and Maclean became suspect. Not until May 1951 was it fairly clear that they were double agents, or moles; and they quickly defected to the Soviet Union one weekend. Philby lingered in the West under a cloud of suspicion; he finally defected in 1963. In 1980 an enterprising British journalist, who had studied the case enough to see where the trail led, identified a fourth man, Sir Anthony Blunt, art historian to the queen, as a Soviet agent. The British government revoked Blunt's knighthood but did nothing else because of the statute of limitations. It was clear, however, that Burgess, Maclean, and Philby long since had made a mockery of Anglo-American secrets of state.

The second part of the K^1C^2 equation—communism—was a serious matter. Senator Joseph R. McCarthy of Wisconsin, who undertook the business of uncovering Communists in the United States, may never have understood how serious it was. President Truman knew that McCarthy was naive in such matters. The senator had never thought about such work until he made a speech to a Republican women's club in Wheeling, West Virginia, on February 9, 1950, and announced that he had in his hand the names of 205 Communists in the U.S. State Department.

Senator McCarthy's most active period in the conspiracy hunt came later, in the first year of the Eisenhower administration, but his speechmaking in the last years of the Truman administration caused grave trouble. McCarthy's figures were imprecise, to say the least; when he went on from Wheeling to speak the next night in Salt Lake City, the stated number of State Department Communists went down from 205 to 57. His technique was also circuitous, never dealing with the accusation of the moment but turning it into something else, meanwhile leaving an ineradicable impression. The president was bitterly angry about McCarthy's activities; he drafted a letter that was never sent but should have been. Indignant that McCarthy should try "to discredit his own Government before the world," he charged, "You know that isn't done by honest public officials." The senator's accusation, he wrote, was not only not true and an insolent approach to a situation that should have been worked out between man and man but it shows conclusively that you are not even fit to have a hand in the operation of the Government of the United States."

It was at about this time that *Washington Post* cartoonist

Herblock coined a new word in American politics—*McCarthyism*; he drew a pile of tar buckets, with the word printed on the big bucket at the top. Short of a knockdown, drag-out fight, however, it was impossible to do anything to McCarthy. The Republicans, including Senator Taft, let him run, believing that, although he might knock down innocent people, he would also find guilty ones. A committee chaired by Senator Millard Tydings of Maryland brought in a report on his activities so adverse that its full acceptance by the Senate would have amounted to censure. The committee report said that McCarthy had failed to substantiate a single case among what he had described as "81 card-carrying Communists in the State Department." The report accused him of "perhaps the most nefarious campaign of half-truths and untruth in the history of this Republic." The senators voted on a motion to censure him according to party lines, however, with a vote in his favor coming even from Margaret Chase Smith of Maine, who earlier had spoken eloquently against conspiracy theories and theorists. The censure vote came out thirty-seven Republicans against, forty-five Democrats in favor, and hence resolved nothing. The Republicans picked up seats in Congress that year, defeating Tydings in Maryland, majority leader Scott Lucas in Illinois, and Representative Helen Gahagan Douglas, who lost in California to the man Truman disliked more than any figure in public life—Richard Nixon. At the height of McCarthy's accusations during the Truman administration, on June 14, 1951, the senator put into the *Congressional Record* a 60,000-word-long diatribe—later reprinted in book form as *America's Retreat from Victory*—charging that General Marshall, who had served as secretary of state and secretary of defense, had failed to stand up to the Communists. McCarthy stated : "I realize full well how unpopular it is to lay hands on the laurels of a man who has been built into a great hero. I very much dislike this unpleasant task, but I feel that it must be done."

The president earlier had set up a loyalty program, to prevent irresponsible accusations after Republican candidates in the

November 1946 elections had run on a pledge to "clean the communists and fellow travelers out of the government." Truman rightly regarded a statutory definition of loyalty as a platform for a witch hunt, so, late in November 1946, he had established a Temporary Commission on Employee Loyalty. The commission brought in a set of recommendations and, based on these recommendations, Truman established the Federal Employee Loyalty Program on March 2, 1947, by Executive Order 9835. The program perhaps was necessary at the time, or some sort of program was necessary—but even relating what happened is embarrassing, for it is difficult to believe that such a program could have gotten under way in the United States in the twentieth century. Truman probably had expected that the program would be better administered, and he later admitted that it "had a lot of flaws." In terms of catching Communists, the program was a failure. By mid-1952, four million persons—employees or prospective employees of the federal government—had undergone at least a routine check. Agency loyalty boards placed tentative charges against 9,077 individuals and held 2,961 formal hearings, from which the administration either dismissed or denied employment to 378 persons—.022 percent of the total. The boards found not a single case of espionage. Beyond the failure to get any results, however, and this was the important failure, was the near total lack of protection for the people investigated. The FBI brought together the testimonies of witnesses who were nothing less than character assassins, and this nonsense was produced at hearings as if it were gospel truth, because it came from the FBI. Character assassins thrived in this atmosphere. As one accused employee, who lost her job, said: " . . . if I am convicted here that will make this person who has made these charges considered a reliable witness; and they are not, because the charges are not true, and whatever is said here should not add to their reliability."

Executive Order 9835 was not enough for McCarthy, nor for other members of the Congress, who feared Communists everywhere, not only in the federal departments. The House and Senate put together their own security program act, under the leadership of Senator Pat McCarran of Nevada, a conservative Democrat. Truman vetoed it, but it passed over his veto on September 23, 1950. The act provided for registration of Communist and Communist-front organizations and for internment of Communists during national emergencies, and it prohibited employment of Communists in national defense work. It prohibited from entry into the United States anyone who had ever been a member of a totalitarian organization. An amendment of March 28, 1951, excepted anyone under age sixteen if that person was forced into a totalitarian organization, or anyone who had joined to maintain his livelihood, if in other respects such an individual was of exemplary character.

By the winter of 1951–1952, the Truman administration was buffeted by conspiracy theories, some of which had a basis in fact, and two real spy rings (Rosenberg-Fuchs and Burgess-Maclean-Philby-Blunt), the most serious in American history to that time. In addition, the Korean War bogged down into savage fighting for unimportant hills in the neighborhood of the thirty-eighth parallel, while truce negotiators haggled over the prisoner exchange. The result of all this was that President Truman found his position distinctly uncomfortable. Memory of the victory in November 1948 had disappeared. In November 1951, a Gallup poll put his popularity at a new low, 23 percent, down from the July 1945 high of 87. (This was similar to the rating of President Nixon in 1974 on the eve of his resignation.) For the rest of Truman's administration, his popularity rating was very low; in January 1953 it had risen only to 31 percent. He had been in bad situations before, however: the primary of 1940; the early months of 1934, when his term as presiding judge was ending and nothing to replace it was in sight; the primary of 1924, when he lost to the harness maker; and early 1922, when the haberdashery was failing and he had no prospect of a job. He was not about to feel sorry for himself. During his long years as a government official, Truman had learned that public opinion of the moment did not count. After he had left Washington and had retired to Independence, he mused one day about polls and pollsters, wondering "how far Moses would have gone if he'd taken a poll in Egypt." What counted, he was sure, was "right and wrong and leadership—men with fortitude, honesty and a belief in the right that makes epochs in the history of the world."

It was not the best of times for Democrats; GOP critics brought up embarrassing episodes of administration improprieties from earlier years and embellished them with stories of corruption in more recent times. In January 1948 the Senate Appropriations Committee had discovered that a friend of the president, Edwin W. Pauley, then special assistant to the secretary of the army, had made several hundred thousand dollars in commodity speculation. Then, the president's physician, "Doc" Graham, was accused of making $6,165 in grain speculation; he was no speculator, but critics jumped up and down in simulated rage. In 1951, a subcommittee of the Senate Banking and Currency Committee headed by Senator Fulbright—whose suggestion that Truman turn over the presidency to the Republicans in 1946 led the president to call him Senator Halfbright—investigated the activities of E. Merl Young, a protégé of Donald Dawson of the White House staff, who had worked for the Reconstruction Finance Corporation and then had taken lucrative jobs with companies that borrowed money from the RFC. In addition, Young's wife worked at the White House and wore a pastel mink coat worth $8,400; Young was friendly with William M. Boyle, Jr., who became chairman of the Democratic national committee in mid-1949; and Young, Dawson, and Boyle were all from Missouri.

There unquestionably were scandals in the Bureau of Internal Revenue, an unfortunate place for scandals because its operations affected all ordinary citizens. The trouble with the bureau was that most of its major officials were political appointees. Secretary Snyder moved rapidly to dismiss errant employees, putting them up for indictment and trial, if necessary. He had purged sixty-six by the end of 1952, including the general counsel of the bureau, Charles Oliphant. Nine of these people went to jail.

Because of the tax scandals, Truman set up a federal commission to investigate corruption in the government and thereby got into more trouble. His choice to head the commission was a New York judge, Thomas F. Murphy, a man of towering bulk and conspicuous mustache who had scourged defense witnesses during the second Hiss trial. Murphy appeared to be interested, but then casually backed away. Truman turned to a Republican with a New York City legal reputation, Newbold Morris, who possessed no political instincts whatsoever. When he was called before a Senate committee, Morris told his interrogators that they had diseased minds. As head of the commission, Morris designed a huge questionnaire for government officials, cabinet members on down, that probably was an invasion of privacy, for it inquired minutely into their sources of income. The president intimated that Attorney General J. Howard McGrath had let Morris get out of hand. McGrath then fired Morris without telling Truman, whereupon Truman picked up the telephone and fired McGrath.

The president looked foolish after firing McGrath. Republicans talked ever more volubly about the mess in Washington. Truman moved effectively against corruption, but when he sought to institutionalize his activity in a commission, his luckless choices gave the impression of total failure. In the ways of Washington, the army of critics that always surrounds the White House began to intensify its attacks.

For Truman, 1952 surely was a time of ill fortune. During a big steel strike, Truman seized the mills, as he had seized the mines in 1946. In April 1952, a federal judge ruled the seizure unconstitutional and ordered the mills returned to the companies, but the next day the circuit court of appeals stayed the order until a judgment by the Supreme Court, which failed to hear the case immediately. Truman called in the president of United States Steel, Benjamin Fairless, and the head of the steelworkers union and the Congress of Industrial Organizations, Philip Murray, and told them: "Gentlemen, the eyes of the nation are upon you. Work out your differences and let's have a settlement." The two men began to talk, but when the Supreme Court announced it would hear the case promptly, negotiation ended. During the ensuing Court hearings, the newspapers attacked the president, and the steel companies took full-page ads castigating him. On June 2, the Court, the chief justice dissenting, upheld the original April decision. The president ever afterward believed that, if the Court had not announced it would take up the case promptly, but had given him a little more time, he could have solved the problem. After the owners took back the mills, 600,000 workers struck for seven weeks, at a cost of $40 million a day. This was right in the middle of the Korean War, and the president finally settled the strike by increasing the price of steel. (It is worth mentioning here that the Supreme Court decisions in *Youngstown Sheet and Tube Company v. Sawyer* in June 1952 and in *United States v. Nixon* in 1974, are the two most important recent Supreme Court decisions limiting the power of the president.)

Meanwhile, the presidential campaign of 1952 was under way, and the Democratic party was in trouble, for General Eisenhower had announced in January that he was a Republican. During that same month, Truman had sensed that the K^1C^2 formula needed a new Democratic chemist to make it dissolve, and he asked Illinois Governor Adlai E. Stevenson to run. Stevenson was extremely reluctant; he spoke about his promises to voters in Illinois as if they precluded translation to national service. Senator Estes Kefauver of Tennessee, who affected a frontier upbringing by wearing a coonskin cap, entered his name against Truman in the New Hampshire primary and beat him decisively. Truman did not like Kefauver, who had irritated Truman beyond measure by going around the country holding hearings on crime in such places as Kansas City (where he began his crime odyssey) and St. Louis, eventually uncovering crime in East St. Louis, Illinois. On March 29, at the Democrats' Jefferson-Jackson Day dinner, the president announced that he was not a candidate. Privately, he almost reconsidered because of Stevenson's coyness, but eventually, at the opening of the Chicago convention that summer, Stevenson called the president and asked if it would embarrass Truman if he went after the nomination. After clearing it with Truman, Stevenson did promptly receive the nomination at the convention.

Stevenson proved to be a wonderful speechmaker but a terrible politician. Off the platform he appeared too intellectual, inspiring an Eisenhower partisan, John Alsop, to coin a word. When John Alsop's brother, the columnist, Stewart Alsop, told him that many Ike supporters were switching to Stevenson, an image came into John Alsop's mind of the sort of person who switched, someone, he said, with "a large oval head, smooth, faceless, unemotional, but a little bit haughty and condescending." John said to Stewart over the telephone, "All the eggheads are for Stevenson." Stevenson sought to distance himself from the Truman administration by establishing campaign headquarters in Springfield, Illinois, and he displaced the able chairman of the Democratic national committee, Frank E. McKinney of Indianapolis, in favor of the untested Chicago lawyer, Stephen A. Mitchell. In response to a series of questions from the *Portland Oregonian*, one asking what he proposed to do about the mess in Washington, he repeated the question, "As for the mess in Washington, . . ." Truman was furious and, in a letter he drafted but did not send, said he would sit out the campaign. He thought that Stevenson was "trying to beat the Democratic President instead of the Republicans and the General of the Army who heads their ticket. There is no mess in Washington . . . I'm telling you to take your crackpots, your high socialites with their noses in the air, run your campaign and win if you can. Cowfever [Kefauver] could not have treated me any more shabbily than have you. . . . Best of luck to you from a bystander who has become disinterested."

Stevenson mended his fences in Washington, and in the last month of the campaign the president took to the hustings, speaking again at the whistlestops, and lambasting the Republican candidate of 1952: "The Republicans have General Motors and General Electric and General Foods and General Mac-Arthur . . . And they have their own five-star general running for President . . . I want to say to you that every general I know is on this list except general welfare, and general welfare is in with the corporals and privates in the Democratic Party."

Ike was unbeatable, however, as soon as he dropped his initially tepid campaign style—crossing the thirty-eighth plati-tude, said reporters—and started to lay it on the line about the Truman administration in accord with Korea, communism, and corruption. On a foray into Wisconsin, he sat on the speaker's platform with Joe McCarthy and excised a tribute in his speech to his old army mentor, General Marshall, failing to notice that his assistants had released the undoctored text of the speech to reporters. Truman was appalled. When the general in a great rally in Detroit seized on a suggestion by his speechwriter Emmet Hughes and announced, "If elected, I will go to Korea," the president was apoplectic, for he knew Ike could do nothing in Korea. Eisenhower won by a landslide.

Harry S. Truman had fought the good fight, and his presi-dency was at last coming to an end. Two months remained between the election and Ike's inaugural, during which Truman ruminated moodily about changes in politics over the years, about his fear for the future of the party he had joined shortly after the turn of the century, and about the awkwardness of having a military man in the White House ("He'll sit here, and he'll say, 'Do this! Do that!' And nothing will happen. Poor Ike! It won't be a bit like the Army. He'll find it very frustrating."). He invited the president-elect to the White House to be briefed on procedures within the executive offices and at the cabinet level. The conference was frosty. A photographer took several pictures of their meeting, and the *New York Times* printed one that showed Truman with a scowl and Eisenhower with a look of boredom. It was the worst picture in the lot, but it caught the spirit of the occasion.

Nevertheless, Truman was sure that the Republic would go

on, that even the Republicans could not turn back the clock—
could not reverse the legislation that had changed the government beginning in 1933 and that, under the Fair Deal, was
accepted by all thinking Americans.

The president and Mrs. Truman, August 5, 1969

VIII

Retirement

IT WAS TIME for Truman to leave the refurbished White House when January 20, 1953, arrived—time to leave the city of Washington, the scene of his life since January 1935. By some measures, the nearly twenty years was a generation—from the middle of the Great Depression, when Franklin D. Roosevelt had not yet served even a single term, until the inaugural day of 1953, when a man became president who had been an army major in 1935 when Truman was a senator. When the day came to go, it was not an occasion to lament, however; to Truman's surprise it turned out to be an occasion to cherish. After the inaugural ceremonies, he had arranged to go to the house of Dean Acheson in Georgetown for a farewell luncheon with the former members of his cabinet. Word of his plan got out, and a huge crowd assembled. The Georgetown street was full of people, who cheered as if he were coming into office instead of going out. The public response was the same at every stop as his train made its way west to Missouri. The train arrived in the Independence station an hour late, at 8:15 P.M., and more than ten thousand people were at the little station—such a crowd and such a jam that no one could get through. Five thousand more people were at the house at 219 North Delaware. "It was the pay-off," Truman wrote in his diary, "for thirty years of hell and hard work."

The former president did not exaggerate. His thirty years in office had been no bed of roses, but the crowds' enthusiasm, especially in Independence, was a reward; Truman, who in retirement liked to describe himself as a retired farmer, never forgot the welcome home. In subsequent days and weeks he rested, and early each morning he took a walk in one direction or another—past the Presbyterian church, or down Van Horn Road (renamed Truman Road during his presidency) to the Baptist Church, taking a cut to the north, perhaps, and then turning west and walking down West Waldo to see the house he had lived in, now remodeled by some new inhabitant who did not like its original Victorian proportions. To the north of the house on West Waldo and River Boulevard was the site of Woodland College, now long since disappeared, where his friend Paul Bryant, son of "Professor" Bryant, had once lived. In place of the college stood a grade school, and on the rest of the land a series of small houses had been built in the 1920s and 1930s. In downtown Independence, the retired farmer saw the rebuilt courthouse, one of the accomplishments of his years as presiding judge, financed out of the bond issue of 1931; Truman had engaged an architect from Shreveport, Louisiana, who had redone the gloomy, railroad-station-style courthouse as a chaste Georgian building, and it looked just like colonial Williamsburg to the president (to all visitors, and to his neighbors, he was known as "the president" after January 20, 1953, just as before). He skirted the aging buildings of the square and sought a vantage point from which to survey the courthouse with its huge four-faced clock.

Truman tried to get out early on his morning walks, but however early he ventured forth, up the alley to the south of the house, a group of onlookers standing across the street would come surging forward to ask him questions, always holding out little pads of paper and cards for his autograph. He gladly obliged, chatting with the onlookers and wishing them well. He shook hands with everyone, even the children. Then he went off on his walk, hoping that no one would follow. To preserve a modicum of privacy, the town furnished him a bodyguard, Mike Westwood, a stolid citizen who was a police officer. In the following years, Mike was seen constantly with the president, walking by his side, carrying a walky-talky in case of trouble. There still were interruptions on the walks, which the president put up with and sometimes even enjoyed, for he realized that, although he sought to think out his problems of the day before or to plan his schedule for the new day, the time had passed when he could stroll as a private citizen and expect not to be bothered. "I still don't feel like a completely private citizen and I don't suppose I ever will," he told a reporter. "It's still almost impossible to do as other people do, even though I've tried. You can't always be as you want to be after you've been under those bright lights."

One time, not long after Truman returned to Independence, a high school student who was running for president of the student council asked to have a picture taken with him, to which the president immediately agreed, although afterward he wondered if it helped or hindered the youthful politician. On another occasion, he met the son of a man he had known years earlier on the farm; without hesitation, and with due pride, the president named off the young man's father and grandfather and told him everything he knew about them, which was a great deal; this, so Truman wrote in his diary, after he had met literally millions of people. It was a good feeling to be home among people he really knew. On still another occasion, an elderly man and woman waved excitedly from across the street; when the president crossed over to talk to them, he discovered that they merely wanted his autograph for their granddaughter, who lived in Detroit and had an autograph book. Truman once came to a place where some work was being done on the street. He stopped and watched the foreman, who did not seem to pay much attention to the president. Eventually, he asked the foreman if he needed a good strawboss. The foreman looked at him, watched the work for a while, and then took another look. He then broke out in a broad smile. "Oh yes!" he said. "You *are* out of a job, aren't you?"

In the first months after leaving office, the president and his wife planned a trip to Hawaii, and late that spring they stayed for

several weeks on the island owned by his friend Ed Pauley. Under
Truman's guidance, Pauley's children and some neighborhood
children formed a coconut cabinet, and the president presided
over his young officialdom, giving them instruction in government. Some years later, for Christmas 1957, Truman arranged
to have specially engraved certificates for his little friends of the
coconut cabinet, crediting them with their acomplishments in
government and other matters, such as short-sheeting and
putting frogs and snakes in beds "and whatever else causes
laughter and ridiculous situations."

When he returned from his Hawaiian trip, the former president
plunged into two educational enterprises, one of which was to
concern him for the rest of his life. The first project was
preparation of his memoirs, which were ready by the autumn of
1955 and published in two volumes that autumn and early the
next spring. The memoirs, composed by the president, were
worked over by several assistants, whose efforts by and large
detracted from the original rather than improving upon it. The
ill proportions of the final manuscript bespoke their cutting to
size after the sprawling first volume, and the work's stolidity
demonstrated the way some of his assistants chopped and
homogenized his prose. Truman was not a dull man and his
approach to life simply did not show through. The memoirs did
show, however, that their author had been busy with an appallingly large number of public matters. In that respect, the
memoirs acquainted their readers with the work of the presidency
in a crucial time.

Even as he was finishing the memoirs, Truman moved into the
middle of a second project, already under way through an
assistant, David D. Lloyd, who was operating in Washington as a
fund gatherer. This second project involved the construction of a
large building in Independence to house Truman's presidential
papers and others, and those of his assistants and members of the
administration. Truman expected the library to constitute a
center for the study of American democracy in action. To design
the library building, Truman appointed a local architect and

friend, Alonzo H. Gentry, assisted by the architect from Shreveport whose Georgian building in the center of Independence he
had admired so often. Apparently the president did not know that
the Shreveport architect had changed this style and was now
designing buildings in a style that could best be described as
Egyptian modern. The eventual library building on part of a
cloverleaf just off U.S. Route 24 looked like nothing so much as
the temple of Queen Hatshepsut across the Nile from Luxor.
Having left the designing to an expert, the president did not
interfere, and came only to admire the new building, which
contained a stack area for manuscripts and a reading area for
researchers, as well as a large museum for memorabilia of the
presidency—the mahogany chairs and table from the Philippines; the huge rug that the young Shah of Iran had given out of
gratitude for Truman's interest in that country; the scimitar and
several ceremonial daggers from old King Ibn Saud of Saudi
Arabia, encrusted with diamonds and rubies, presented in
appreciation of the services of Doc Graham, who had removed a
benign tumor from the monarch's throat. Millions of Americans
saw the exhibits. Unfortunately, at 6:30 A.M. on March 24, 1978,
thieves broke in, hacked the scimitar and daggers out of their case
in the foyer, and made off with a fortune in jewels.

The library became the second of several presidential libraries.
The custom had been inaugurated by President Roosevelt, who
before his death arranged to have a building constructed near his
house at Hyde Park—to avoid paying for maintenance of the
estate, some critics said. Later presidential libraries included the
Hoover library in West Branch, Iowa; the Eisenhower Library in
Abilene, Kansas; the Kennedy Library in Boston; the Johnson
Library in Austin, Texas; the Ford Library in Ann Arbor,
Michigan; and the Carter Library in Atlanta. None fulfilled the
hopes of the founders, least of all Truman, who hoped to provide
a regional center for presidential studies, to be used by students
from the neighboring states of Iowa, Nebraska, Kansas, Oklahoma, Arkansas, and Illinois. Truman's presidential papers did
prove fascinating to researchers, however, especially when the

diary and private memoranda and marvelously informative and
rambunctious letters, sent and unsent, were opened late in the
1970s. Truman's papers turned out to be the best private
presidential papers of the twentieth century.

During his years of retirement, political matters often occupied
the former president's days. The 1950s were a quiet time
internationally, although there were problems—such as the Suez
crisis in 1956, when the Egyptians occupied the canal and the
British and French conspired with the Israelis to take it back,
causing a great crisis in which the United States and the Soviet
Union lined up against the British and the French in the United
Nations and forced them to evacuate their forces from Egypt. In
1958, there was a crisis in Lebanon, when fear that the Egyptians,
under the charismatic Gamal Abdel Nasser, might take over
Lebanon led to a temporary occupation of that little country by a
division of U.S. Marine and U.S. Army troops. Difficulties
continued with the Soviet Union, and, although the Geneva
summit conference of 1955 momentarily brought together the
leaders of the big four—the United States, Britain, France, and the
USSR—rivalries of earlier years were compounded in 1960 by the
shooting down of an American spy plane, a U-2 (Utility-2)
reconnaissance jet, caught flying over the industrial city of
Sverdlovsk. In domestic political affairs, the 1950s saw an
increasing concern for black civil rights and the beginnings of a
black revolution. In the late 1950s construction of the interstate
highway system began and also the building of more suburbs,
more houses, more apartment buildings—the stretching out of
urban America into the countryside that came with increasing
affluence and increasing population. Observing the swirl of
affairs, foreign and domestic, the retired president became ever
more convinced that the Republicans were merely taking things
as they came and were concerned not for the majority of
Americans but only for the privileged. He feared that the
Republican party was trying to turn the clock back to the 1920s,
the era of Harding and Coolidge and Hoover, when the govern-

ment in Washington watched the domestic economy and foreign affairs cascade toward disaster.

The Eisenhower years, which so enchanted millions of Americans, did not enchant Harry Truman. Eisenhower had seemed harmless enough as the general who presided over the victorious coalition in Europe. When he had gone to Europe early in 1951 to bring the NATO forces together in a workable organization, Truman still had favorable feelings toward him. Ike's entry into the presidential race in 1952 was something else, however, and his actions in office appalled Truman. He was careful not to criticize Eisenhower during great foreign upheavals such as Suez and Lebanon, but privately he was highly uncertain of Ike's abilities to handle large international problems. As for domestic problems, he was absolutely certain that the Republicans, led by the amiable general-president, were giving away the birthright of the American people in exchange for what Eisenhower described as dynamic or modern Republicanism.

Truman always believed that the Democratic party was the party of the people and that the Republicans were economic royalists. He wanted the Republican party to be strong enough to keep the Democrats on their toes and strong enough to stand up so that it could be knocked down every other year and knocked out every fourth year. For this grand purpose, the retired president made himself available as a speechmaker and traveled from place to place, from Atlantic to Pacific, from north to south, supporting local Democratic candidates and shoring up national figures so as to minimize factionalism. The president believed that the duty of a politician was to show loyalty to the party that had helped him; he detested bolters such as the Republicats, as he labeled the Dixiecrats. In the 1950s, however, when he was most active as a party leader, he found the party in a shambles because of the amateurish efforts of Stevenson.

In the 1960s a new set of international and national problems arose that were far more serious than those of preceding years. The attempted United States invasion of Cuba in 1961 failed

abysmally, and was followed the next year by the missile crisis—
the Russian attempt to emplace nuclear missiles in Cuba that
threatened the entire eastern United States as far as the Mississippi. The specter of Vietnam loomed in the middle of the
1960s and soon mesmerized Americans. On the domestic front,
affairs seemed to be in order, with the Democrats pushing more
and more social programs through Congress in the name of the
New Frontier of John F. Kennedy's administration and the Great
Society of Lyndon B. Johnson.

The progress of events in the 1960s, foreign and domestic, was
out of the hands of the retired president, and from the middle of
the decade he could no longer fix his attention upon them even if
he had wished. At the end of the 1950s, the Democratic party
passed into the hands of people who were strangers to Truman—
supporters of Kennedy. Younger members of the party considered Truman and his confederate Acheson to be old men and
claimed that they represented the Democrats of the nineteenth
century and that it was time for a change. When change came in
1960, with Kennedy, Truman was so disgruntled by the choice of
someone he considered a boy for president that, for the first time
in many years, he did not attend the party convention. Kennedy's
Catholicism did not bother Truman; as a good Baptist he had
long admired Monsignor Tiernan, his neighbor in Kansas City,
who had been chaplain of the 129th Field Artillery in World War
I. At the funeral of Roy Muehlebach, the president had sat next to
Monsignor George W. King, who offered to say a mass for him;
Truman told the monsignor that he could use several. His
reservations about Kennedy were not so much a problem of the
Pope but of Kennedy's father, for Truman considered Joseph P.
Kennedy an economic royalist. He later warmed to President
Kennedy, and in 1961 he visited the White House for the first time
since he had left it in 1953. He did not warm to Attorney General
Robert F. Kennedy, who refused to move quickly in pardoning
his one-time presidential appointments secretary, Matthew J.
Connelly, who had been convicted of income tax evasion in what
Truman believed was a prejudiced trial presided over by one of

his political enemies. He wrote to the younger Kennedy, telling him not to come around smiling at him again until he had done his duty by Matt.

In the early 1960s, the retired farmer seemed to be running along just as he had, without let-up. He had gone to Europe on a long trip in 1956, after Margaret's marriage to the New York newspaperman Clifton T. Daniel, and had seen enough of it to be sure that he liked the United States much better, although he had always known he did. In 1958, he and Bess went to Europe again, with Judge and Mrs. Samuel I. Rosenman, and spent weeks in Italy and on the French Riviera; this was a more private trip. In 1964, in his eighty-first year, he flew with his son-in-law and a select group of mourners to the funeral of the king of Greece, and enjoyed seeing the Acropolis, after having read many years before about it and the other treasures of Greece.

The president was slowing down, however, if ever so imperceptibly, and in 1964, in a fall in the upstairs bathroom on Delaware Street, after stubbing his toe on the raised floor off the hall, he struck his head and was badly shaken. He never fully recovered from the fall. Loss of weight made him look drawn and thin, pitifully frail. His eyes, which had always been weak, looked enormous and staring behind thick lenses, and his hearing was bad. His sister Mary Jane worried. "He doesn't look a thing like he used to," she said. "He always had a full face and always looked so well. He takes a miserable picture now, he's so thin. And he's always taken such a nice picture." He continued to receive visitors occasionally, and once in a while he went to his office in the library. It was not like the earlier years, when he was there every morning, about 6:30 or 7:00, sometimes earlier, depending on when his walk ended. The walks continued with Mike Westwood, but the pace was much slower—no longer the 120 steps to the minute that he had learned in the army in 1917–1919.

The retired president took ever more solace in books, spending much of his time sitting in a huge chair in the reading room of the house, where bookshelves covered the walls from floor to ceiling on three sides and over the window on the fourth. When he ran out of books at home, he went to the public library. The Trumans' light green Chrysler could be seen pulling out of the driveway on the North Delaware side: Mike driving, the president next to him on the front passenger seat, clasping a cane between his knees, Bess in back, and the secret service car discreetly behind. When the car arrived at the library, Bess went inside and gathered an armload of books. Then the president went back home to the reading room chair. The artist Tom Benton painted him in that chair—a portrait that startled friends. The portrait showed a white-haired old man engrossed in a book held in gnarled, arthritic fingers. His shirt collar and suit were loose; his nose was hawk-like. "The old man looks better as an old man than he did as a young man," Benton said. "You get that fat off of him and you see that chicken-hawk face and also his sensitivity. . . . You didn't ever see the real man, you saw only the mask."

In 1969, Truman barely managed a public appearance at home and in the library with the new president of the United States, Richard Nixon, the man he always believed had called him a traitor in 1952 and whom he, in turn, had dubbed "squirrel-head." When this man became president of the United States and chose to visit Independence, Truman paid his respects, not to the man but to the office. Thereafter, he kept to the house and saw only a few close friends, such as Ed Pauley, who came to call with his wife years after the time of the coconut cabinet. Finally, it became impossible for him to keep going in the house, and the president went to the hospital in Kansas City. He managed to survive Christmas Day 1972 but died twenty-four hours later, at the age of eighty-eight.

The Oval Office

IX

The Modern American Presidency

THREE SPECIAL POINTS about the life of Harry S. Truman remain to be related. The first is the manner in which he transformed the office of president of the United States, making it into the institution we know today. The second subject is the personal qualities he displayed in the nation's highest office, which ensured his success as president. The final point involves the contemporary misjudgment of his greatness when he was president—the fact that many Americans, judging by the polls an overwhelming majority, chose to believe that he was anything but a great man, that he was in fact a very small man who rose to the presidency by luck, by happenstance.

In retrospect, it is fascinating to observe the manner in which Truman took hold of the presidency and transformed it. He knew that the presidency was the most powerful office in the world if he managed it properly; he had to make the bureaucracy do his bidding, or he would be president only in name. For a decade, he had lived in Washington and had seen the workings of the Senate, a congenial club where faithful members got ahead, although the Senate had its share of do-nothings and blowhards and people with more ambition than loyalty to constituents and country. In the same decade, he had developed an acquaintance with the Supreme Court. One of his staff members had introduced him to Justice Louis D. Brandeis, and the senator and the justice instantly became friends, each sensing the other's idealism. They shared an interest in economics, which was not an abstract science to them; both men had studied the role of railroads in American life, and during the war they had watched the way the economy responded to patriotism. For Truman, however, the Court stood apart from the hurly-burly of government, and Congress and the president did the work. Beginning in April 1945, he considered his job to be making the presidency effective.

The new president was well aware of the tremendous changes in his office during the terms of Roosevelt, the first modern American president. In earlier times the office had little pretentiousness; the man who happened to be president lived like other citizens of the Republic. John Adams's wife Abigail hung up washing in the unfinished East Room. President William Henry Harrison went shopping for his wife and carried his own basket. Administratively, matters were simple; Abraham Lincoln was assisted by only two secretaries, John G. Nicolay and John Hay. In the 1880s, the White House had only one telephone, and in the evenings Grover Cleveland answered it. The duties of the president were not time-consuming. Neither Theodore Roosevelt nor Wilson worked very hard, for the office did not require it. Teddy Roosevelt played a great deal and loved to travel. Until the outbreak of the war in 1917, Wilson worked three or four hours a day and, according to his chief usher Irwin H. (Ike) Hoover, "spent much of his time happily and quietly, sitting around with his family." Calvin Coolidge slept thirteen hours a day, taking afternoon snoozes in the Oval Office. Herbert Hoover was the last of the old-time presidents. By the time Roosevelt took over in the midst of the Great Depression, the American people were demanding a strong presidency. It was essential for the administration of the New Deal and equally essential during World War II.

Truman's criticism of Roosevelt's administration was not about the size of the mechanism—cabinet departments, White House staff, executive office staff—but that FDR had established no clear lines of control. The number of cabinet departments had not increased since before World War I, when there were ten, and their size seemed sensible, although State, War, and

Navy appeared labyrinthine. A large White House staff surely was necessary, and Truman did not object to its growth from thirty-seven people in March 1933 to several times that many in 1945. He approved of the new Executive Office of the President, created in 1939. He did not mind the president taking on the role of manager; he believed that Roosevelt had not managed well. Roosevelt gave the impression of being a master organizer; someone said he organized a circle, with himself at the hub. In fact, he managed his cabinet and White House staff and executive office staff by allowing everything to sprawl and then trying to control and manipulate the jumble—or jungle—in complicated ways. He paid little attention to the cabinet, often appointing incompetents and sycophants as Truman thought, and preferred to do the government's work by dealing with undersecretaries and assistant secretaries or through notes to lower officials. Roosevelt was fond of imposing new layers of bureaucracy on old ones or transferring bureaus. Assistants with vague responsibilities operated from the White House or executive office staffs. The president pushed subordinates into fights just to see the feathers fly, although the public thought he thereby beheld the competing positions and chose his own. One of FDR's minor officials, Assistant Secretary of State Dean Acheson, wrote years later that what looked like chaos was indeed chaos.

When Truman took office, his first order of business was to establish authority over the cabinet. A few years later, when Roosevelt's last press secretary, Jonathan Daniels, was finishing what Truman hoped would be a truthful book about his administration, a volume published in 1950 under title of *The Man of Independence*, Truman wrote Daniels a letter about the Roosevelt cabinet, which he never sent. The president said that FDR's cabinet was an impossible group of incompetents, prima donnas, and disloyal men, who were more interested in themselves than in the public welfare. Secretary of State Edward R. Stettinius, Jr., he said, was "a fine man, good looking, amiable, cooperative, but never had an idea new or old." He claimed that

Secretary of Labor Frances Perkins was an estimable woman but "no politician. F.D.R. had removed every bureau and power she had." Secretary of the Treasury Henry Morgenthau, Jr., considered himself expert on foreign relations as well as finance and was the author of the Morgenthau Plan to "pastoralize," that is, deindustrialize, Germany. He had told Truman in the early summer of 1945 that he wanted to attend the Potsdam Conference and would resign if he could not attend; the president took him at his word and ushered him out of office. Truman said that Morgenthau was a "blockhead, nut—I wonder why F.D.R. kept him around." The president also had asked Attorney General Francis Biddle to leave, replacing him with an assistant, Tom Clark. Secretary of Agriculture Claude Wickard, "a nice man, who never learned how his department was set up," gave way to Clinton P. Anderson. Within three months, Truman had retired six of the ten Roosevelt department heads.

Then, in the spring of 1946 and again in late summer of that year, came the forced resignations of Secretary of the Interior Ickes and Secretary of Commerce Wallace. According to Truman, " 'Honest' Harold Ickes . . . was never for anyone but Harold, would have cut F.D.R.'s throat—or mine for his 'high minded' ideas of a headline—and did." As for Wallace, he had "no reason to love me or to be loyal to me. Of course he wasn't loyal." Both resignations were to the credit of the president, but he handled them in untidy ways, although perhaps no one could have handled such messes easily. The resignations splashed across the front pages as if the president had asked these two illustrious men to do impossible tasks and they in all honor had declined and left public office. Both men had courted dismissal. Ickes foolishly had opposed the nomination of Ed Pauley as undersecretary of the navy, insinuating that Pauley, an oilman, would sell or lease oil lands just as had President Warren G. Harding's secretary of the navy, Edwin L. Denby, in the early 1920s. Later, Ickes apologized, and he supported Truman in 1948. Wallace's firing was even more justified. During a short interview in Truman's office he trapped the president into a quick perusal of the draft of a long speech. The president trusted him, and the secretary of commerce gave the speech in Madison Square Garden, claiming that Truman had approved what turned out to be a policy toward the Soviet Union very different from that which Secretary of State Byrnes was following in negotiation with the Russians in Paris. Furthermore, in his speech, Wallace departed from his text by omitting sentences critical of the USSR and by inserting sentences friendlier than those Truman had read. Truman was forced to admit that, when he said he had "read every word" of the speech, he had really only leafed through it. Secretary Byrnes threatened to resign, and after a lapse of time during which the president hoped for an exit from his dilemma, he fired Wallace.

There were other cabinet changes over the years, including three changes in the Department of State—Byrnes, General Marshall, and Acheson. Truman replaced Secretary of Defense James V. Forrestal with Louis Johnson, who was replaced by Marshall and then by Robert A. Lovett. Ultimately, twenty-four men served as cabinet officers. Four of the first half-dozen were or had been congressmen. After Morgenthau's successor, Fred Vinson, became chief justice of the Supreme Court, an Arkansas banker and long-time National Guard friend of the president, John W. Snyder, took his place. Julius A. Krug replaced Ickes, but his faint enthusiasm in the 1948 election caused Truman to give the interior job to Undersecretary Oscar Chapman. Truman also promoted an assistant secretary of agriculture, Brannan, to the cabinet.

Sam Rayburn's much-quoted remark about Truman—that he was right on all the big things, wrong on all the little ones—was not really true about the cabinet, to which the president made many good appointments. It certainly was true that for State and Defense, with the exception of Johnson, his choices were first-rate. When the president made a bad appointment, he moved to correct it—unlike Roosevelt, who had kept Secretary of State Cordell Hull around for twelve years. The president forced Johnson's resignation with a notable lack of tact. "Come in,

Lou," he said to the waiting defense secretary, "I have to ask for your resignation."

The president's second order of business in establishing his administration, which he accomplished simultaneously with getting control of the cabinet, was to set up an efficient White House staff. He organized it along traditional lines—secretaries for press, correspondence, and appointments, plus a few special assistants. As press secretary, he inherited Daniels, son of President Wilson's secretary of the navy, Josephus Daniels. The younger Daniels was by profession and temperament a writer; he was not suited to the hustle of a White House office, and Truman replaced him with Charlie Ross. By 1945, Ross was a lanky, cigarette-smoking newspaperman; he was the same age as the president and hence deemed too old for the job, but his was a good appointment. Though sometimes slow-moving, Charlie knew the ways of journalism from his years with the *Post-Dispatch*. Moreover, he could walk into the president's office with the familiarity of a half-century. Upon his appointment, he and the president called their old high school teacher, Miss Tillie Brown, in Independence. In 1901, Miss Tillie had given Charlie a kiss after graduation, because he was valedictorian, while the other boys stood around. "Don't we get any?" they had asked. "Not until you've earned it," said Miss Tillie. When the president and Charlie called to tell of the appointment, Harry asked for the kiss. When Ross died of a heart attack in 1950, his position passed to Joseph H. Short, Jr., and upon Short's death in 1952 to Roger Tubby.

As secretary for correspondence, Truman kept Roosevelt's appointee, William D. (Bill) Hassett, a white-haired, courtly New Englander known as "the Bishop." His job was to compose fancy letters for correspondents whose queries were not worth the president's personal attention and also to compose proclamations for such occasions as Love Your Dog Week and other formal occasions for which people solicited the president's attention. Bill Hassett had a way with words and did well with his duties, but his job became very routine, because Rose A.

Conway, a prim spinster from Missouri, took care of the president's private letters, and because Bill took too much solace from alcohol and was away from his White House desk for weeks on end.

Matt Connelly became the third of Truman's major secretaries, his appointments secretary. This slim, tall, black-haired, handsome Boston Irishman, a staff member of Truman's Senate investigating committee, kept tabs on the legions of people, important and otherwise, who desired to see the president. Connelly promised and procrastinated and sagely kept the traffic moving in and out of the Oval Office, which was not easy when every appointee was ready and eager to hold the president's attention.

In addition to the three traditional secretaries, the president appointed John R. Steelman—known as Dr. Steelman because of his Ph.D. in economics and sociology from the University of North Carolina—as the assistant to the president, the definite article showing his precedence over the several special assistants. Steelman handled labor problems, as Jimmy Byrnes had done for FDR. There was much labor trouble in the first part of Truman's presidency. Moreover, Truman made a poor appointment as secretary of labor—his friend Lewis B. Schwellenbach, former senator from Washington—and he needed a pinch hitter. Steelman also handled federal agency programs and policies, serving as the route to the president for minor agencies that did not have direct access to the Oval Office.

Two other special assistants of the Truman era were Donald S. Dawson, coordinator for personnel and patronage, who maintained files from which Truman made appointments save for customs houses and federal courts; and David Niles, a holdover from the Roosevelt staff, whose responsibility was minority groups.

In 1943, President Roosevelt had created the anomalous office of special counsel for his speechwriter and political savant, Judge Sam Rosenman. When the judge left the White House in 1946, Truman appointed his then naval aide, the handsome young Missouri lawyer Clark Clifford, to that office. Clifford was an excellent choice, for he had his roots in the right place, having made his mark in practice in St. Louis before going into the navy. Clifford was just the man to deal with legal awkwardnesses in congressional bills and executive orders and also to give even better political advice than Sam Rosenman had given. The special counsel handled the president's stable of speechwriters and served as liaison with the Pentagon and the State Department. Clifford returned to private practice in 1950, becoming the most influential lawyer in Washington during the next generation, and he was secretary of defense under President Lyndon B. Johnson in 1968–1969, when he helped persuade Johnson to end the Vietnam War. His place as special counsel to Truman went to one of Truman's special assistants, Charles S. Murphy, an equally competent man, who did not, however, continue Clifford's responsibility for coordination of national security.

In the initial weeks of Truman's administration, the coordination of this melange of White House secretaries and assistants was casual, some assistant or other bringing a problem to the president, but it became apparent that the best way to handle staff matters was to hold morning conferences. Thereafter, the three traditional secretaries and other assistants sat around the president's desk for a half-hour beginning at 9:00 A.M. each morning, and Truman parceled out his business and went around the circle for their business. Among those present was the assistant press secretary, Eben A. Ayers, who, unknown to the group, kept a daily diary that recorded the sessions in detail.

Truman's White House staff eventually numbered a dozen principal secretaries and assistants and several dozen subordinate aides—285 in 1952. By 1972 the staff had grown to 52 secretaries and assistants and 550 subordinates. By 1980, the total of principal advisers and lesser staff members declined to 384.

At the time and later, people argued that Truman brought in a new "White House gang" in 1945, similar to Harding's friends a quarter-century earlier. New faces appeared in the executive offices, but the group hardly looked like Harding's poorer appointees. Truman's staff appointees were generally good and frequently excellent. The only two individuals around the Truman White House who might have detracted from the environment were Major General Harry H. Vaughan, Truman's military aide, and George E. Allen, a roly-poly official who had been present in the Roosevelt years as an administrator of the District of Columbia and who became an intimate of Truman's successor, President Eisenhower. Allen was a quiet fellow, and the press noted his presence mostly on presidential boat trips up and down the Potomac. He was a raconteur and was pleasant to have around. So was Vaughan, whom the president had known since World War I, when Vaughan, then a second lieutenant, had walked unwittingly into an altercation involving First Lieutenant Harry S. Truman and Brigadier General Lucien G. Berry. Vaughan's presence took the heat off the occasion, and Truman was grateful. Afterward, the two men saw a good deal of each other, and Vaughan became an assistant in Truman's senatorial and vice-presidential office, except during the war years, when he served in the South Pacific. An improbable military figure, Vaughan traversed the ranks from colonel to major general during his years with Truman and talked loosely about his influence with "the Boss," thereby making himself known to newspapermen as a one-man gang.

The executive office staff that Truman inherited from Roosevelt consisted of the Bureau of the Budget and a collection of emergency panels, specialized agencies, and policy councils, from before the war and wartime, together with an interesting theoretical framework set out in the report of the President's Committee on Administrative Management in 1937 and the Executive Office of the President, created by Congress in 1939. The 1937 committee, chaired by Louis Brownlow, had included the eminent political scientist from the University of Chicago, Charles E. Merriam, and the well-known expert in public administration, Luther Gulick. Its keynote, announced in its report, was "The President needs help," and its solution was what one student described as a plan of salvation by staff; that is, the committee concluded that not only should the White House have an augmentation of six special assistants "possessed of high competence, great vigor, and a passion for anonymity," but the president also needed a second administrative group, the executive office staff. The most important part of the executive staff in 1939 was the Budget Bureau, which had been transferred from the Treasury Department; it had a staff of forty. In 1939, the combined White House and executive office staffs numbered 800 people, and most of these people were executive office staff. By the time Truman became president, the executive staff had grown by leaps and bounds. The Budget Bureau alone had 500 people. By 1980, when it was known as the Office of Management and Budget, it had 656 staff members. Statistics for executive office staff totals over the years are difficult to obtain, as people often came in temporarily from cabinet departments and other agencies. It is known that by 1952, however, the executive staff numbered 1,166. By the early 1970s, the staff had gone beyond 5,000, but in 1980 it dropped to 1,500.

An addition to the executive office staff in the Truman years was the Council of Economic Advisers (CEA), a three-man panel of trained economists, which had been foisted on the executive office by Congress in 1946, in hope that the president would use it. The Great Depression had taught many economic lessons, and the war had been instructive. Congress and economists believed that conversion from war to peace needed guidance, and the possibility of managing the economy was attractive. Truman's first CEA chairman, the conservative Edwin A. Nourse, felt that the president ignored him, although he perhaps should not have expected the chief executive to spend time in long economic discussions when the budget was only one of Truman's responsibilities. Nourse sensed that the president preferred the counsel of his two liberal colleagues, especially the ebullient Leon Keyserling, who became Nourse's successor in

1949. Keyserling never lacked for words and opinions, and he believed his influence much larger than Nourse's.

Truman also received economic advice from his director of the budget, Harold D. Smith, until June 1946, and from Smith's successors. Smith did not appeal to the president—Truman thought him an "A-1 conniver"—but his successors pleased the president.

It is interesting that no rivalry appeared between directors of the budget and the CEA, even though staff members frequently moved from one office to the other. The result was that Truman received better economic advice than any previous president had received. His administration did not need the economic hunches that marked FDR's administration. Truman himself helped in the budget work by looking for congressional and military maneuvering; because of his years of experience in the Senate, he was expert at hunting it down.

The executive office staff changed under Truman because of the addition not merely of the CEA but also of the National Security Council (NSC), with its system for advising the president created by the National Security Act of 1947 and its 1949 amendments. The primary purpose of this legislation was to unify the military, putting it under a single head so as to analyze military functions and assign each to whatever service could best handle it, rather than allowing two or three services to compete for scarce funds. The army and navy each persisted in maintaining planes and pilots in competition with the air force. The mission of the B-36, a huge propeller-driven bomber, raised questions about the navy's maintenance of huge aircraft carriers. The 1947 act put the secretaryships of war and the navy on a subcabinet level, created a secretaryship of the air force, and imposed a new cabinet office and officer—the Department of Defense and its secretary. Forrestal, appointed from the navy department in 1947, failed to control his subcabinet secretaries, thinking that he could talk them into acting like subordinates. The president brought General Dwight D. Eisenhower down to

Washington from Columbia University on a part-time basis to control the generals and admirals, but they too proved uncontrollable. Years passed before the Defense Department had enough staff.

The National Security Council was at first a purely advisory, moribund body that talked only to itself—rather, its members' deputies talked to each other. Its original members were the president (as chairman), the secretary of state, the secretary of defense, the three military service secretaries, and other department or agency heads. The 1949 amendments dropped the service secretaries and added the vice-president. The permanent staff of the NSC was small, reaching seventy in 1980; as in the case of the executive office staff, however, the NSC borrowed people from Defense, State, and other departments. Initially, Truman absented himself from NSC meetings, perhaps out of fear that he might make instant commitments. He also may have thought that the NSC might inject itself between him and the cabinet departments. He excused himself by saying that members could speak more freely if he were not present. He made the decision to intervene in Korea in 1950 without consulting the NSC; but that war convinced him that he could put the NSC to greater use, and he began to meet with it weekly, forming a supercabinet.

A major Truman contribution to the modern American presidency came in 1947, after Congress sent up a bill, which the president signed, establishing a Commission on the Organization of the Executive Branch of the Government. The Republican Eightieth Congress sensed victory in 1948, and one of the act's objectives was "defining and limiting executive functions." To Congress's surprise, Truman greeted this GOP move with enthusiasm and, in a master stroke, appointed as chairman an impeccable Republican, his friend Herbert Hoover. The president liked Hoover, enjoyed working with him, and already had given him assignments surveying world food supplies. He was glad to pass this organizational task to the party patriarch, who was himself delighted with such congenial work. Unleashing his prodigious energy, Hoover served as his own staff director and put his imprint on all the commission's activities. The first of nineteen reports of the Hoover Commission appeared in 1949. The independent Hoover wanted more power in the White House, and it was Truman's turn to be delighted. According to a close student of presidential organization, Stephen Hess, Hoover—the last person to be president before the modern era—"had come out of retirement to legitimate the Rooseveltian concept of the presidency. It was symbolism of some potency." The press and Congress took up Hoover's proposals, and the president signed them into law.

Such are the ways in which Truman developed the modern American presidency. Beginning in 1933, the nation beheld a huge growth of the executive branch. The federal government increased from 600,000 civilian employees in 1932 to 2,600,000 twenty years later, with 4,000 in the judicial branch, 22,500 in the legislative, and 2,570,000 in the executive (1,300,000 in defense, 500,000 in the post office, the rest in other activities). It would have been fatuous to try to direct such a bureaucracy from the White House and executive office staffs, however large they might have been. Neither, incidentally, could the president control the bureaucracy through appointments, for most civilian employees were under civil service; of the 2,570,000 employees in the executive branch, the president had appointed only 3,000. Truman therefore kept his authority within cabinet departments. It was necessary to check up, to watch to see that policy was carried out, but he had to delegate supervision to the cabinet.

Admittedly, there was increased use of presidential staff members as advisers, leading to suspicions that the bureaucracy was going slowly on reforms desired by the president and thus to a willingness to impose new layers of management. Truman engaged in far less of this activity than his predecessor had, and one characteristic of the modern American presidency that he carefully avoided was use of presidential assistants as special pleaders, as representatives of citizen groups or of possible projects, although his White House staff looked to the future when he appointed David Niles as an administrative assistant with responsibility for minorities. He would have shuddered to behold what came of that Roosevelt innovation—turning the White House into a place for special pleaders. President Nixon's White House staff, for example, contained administrative assistants for the aged, youth, women, blacks, Jews, labor, Hispanic-Americans, the business community, governors and mayors, artists, and citizens of the District of Columbia, and for such concerns as drug abuse, energy, environment, physical fitness, volunteerism, telecommunications, and national goals.

Under Truman, the White House and executive office staffs did not manage business with the clockwork precision that came with his successor, Eisenhower, but Truman did not want Republican precision. When President-elect Eisenhower visited White House offices in November 1952 and the president instructed him on procedure in the Oval Office, Ike horrified Truman by asking who was Truman's chief of staff. The president managed to say without sarcasm that he had no chief of staff, but the very notion that someone should stand between him and presidential administration bothered him; he considered it another piece of military nonsense. The presidency functioned well under Eisenhower; staff duties were sharply defined, and staff assistants got together before entering the president's office and decided on common points rather than offering a choice. Eisenhower wanted things that way. Governor Sherman Adams of New Hampshire served as his chief of staff until a cloud of suspicion passed over the governor because he had accepted hotel accommodations and a vicuña coat from a Massachusetts mill owner who was having tax trouble. After Adams's fall, Eisenhower thoughtfully divided the duties of chief of staff. There was some invisible looseness in Ike's table of organization, however, such as the anomalous role of his press secretary, James Hagerty, who was the president's hatchetman in Congress, especially for the errant Senator McCarthy.

Presidents after Truman and Eisenhower lost control of the

cabinet, or ignored it, which was the same thing. By creating or continuing elephantine White House and executive office staffs, they lost control of that management mechanism. In desperation, they turned the presidency into an organ of public relations.

President Harry S. Truman

X

Qualities of Greatness

IF A SINGLE TRAIT could be credited with making Truman a great president, it was his modesty. He was an extraordinarily modest man. He knew that he, Harry S. Truman, only happened to occupy the presidency, and that, when people made a fuss over him, sometimes embarrassing him, they did it not for his sake, but to pay their respects to the office. He carefully drew a distinction between himself and the office.

His Baptist faith also helped him keep his head. There was a streak of experimentation in the Truman blood; in 1890 his mother had sent him to Presbyterian Sunday School because she had tired of what she considered the hypocrites and unbelievers in one of the rural Baptist churches. Presbyterianism did not appeal to him, however, and Truman became a member of the Baptist church in Grandview and kept his membership there, even when he lived in Independence, where the First Baptist Church was two blocks down Van Horn Road (named for a Republican, renamed Truman Road to his everlasting annoyance). When the Grandview Baptists gave up their old place of worship and constructed a new, modern edifice that the president privately thought resembled a funeral parlor, he nonetheless went out and helped to dedicate it, to the glory of God, he hoped. His wife belonged to the Episcopal Church. They were married in the little Episcopal chapel in Independence, and he frequently went there with Bess, but the bishops bothered him. In the White House, he had to receive some, whom he described in his diary as "High Bishops Episcopal."

He had little patience for the two who came to ask him not to appoint an official representative to the Vatican because an ambassador would erase the necessary line between church and state in favor of the Church of Rome. Some of the president's friends in the Church of Rome, such as Monsignor Tiernan, were much more attractive to him than the "High Bishops Episcopal." Mainly, however, he liked the Baptist church because it interposed no intermediary between him and God. Truman prayed every morning, always the same prayer, and had done so since in his teens; it was a prayer for humility. He did not attend church every Sunday, and during his presidency churchgoing became an ordeal. He could see all the eyes looking at him, even when he sat quietly in the pew. He was a devout Baptist and did not want a church service turned into a circus, with himself in the center ring.

Another source of Truman's humility was the influence of his family. His wife, Bess W. Truman, as she signed herself (she disliked her given name of Elizabeth, and patiently tolerated her husband's epistolary "Miss Lizzie"), was a down-to-earth individual who did what politics required of her, such as "shaking paws" at receptions and having large groups of visiting women in to White House teas (sometimes two or three teas an afternoon). She disliked ceremony and the goldfish-bowl aspect of life as the First Lady, however, and whenever she could she packed her bags and those of her aging mother and arranged to go back to Independence by train. There she remained for weeks or months, painting the inside of the house and, with her long-time helper Vietta Garr, washing all the curtains. "The Boss," as Truman described Mrs. Truman, took no nonsense from anyone and acted as a balance wheel for any untoward behavior by her presidential husband. The president's family was equally down-to-earth; for them the taking on of airs by their relative the president would have been impossible. Across from the Truman house in Independence lived the Noland sisters and their mother, Aunt Ella. In Kansas City were Vivian and his wife Luella, transplanted farm folks. Vivian had four boys and a girl, and to them the president was Uncle Harry. In Grandview were Mary Jane and the president's mother (until her death in 1947). Mary Jane once testified to the need to be one's self: "As Mamma said," she told a newspaperman, "just be in the key of B-natural, and that's what all of us have always been. We didn't pretend anything we were not."

Finally, and if only for the sake of his daughter Margaret, the president would never have considered himself an important person. He had tried for years, ever since he was Judge Truman, to keep Margaret's hopes and purposes simple and unaffected, and the last thing he wanted to come out of his presidency was a feeling on her part that she was better than other people because of her father's position. Margaret's down-to-earth qualities were essential, the president said to himself and to his wife. He watched her to be sure she was not moving away from her upbringing as a home girl who sang each Sunday in the church choir.

In addition to modesty, derived from the president's view of his office, his religion, and his family, Truman possessed a remarkably keen analytical ability, which came partly from inheritance but also from the long years of dealing with people and their problems. Some of it resulted from his experience in the bank, some from trying to make ends meet while living on the farm from 1906 to 1917, a good deal from his military experience of 1917–1919, more from a decade of work on the county court, and yet more from the decade in the Senate. In everything Truman did as president, he tried to look at problems coldly, impartially, and without personal or ideological bias, so as to discern the shortest route between two points. Here his modesty helped, for he did not see problems through the lens of his own importance; he could take himself out of the equation and peer at difficulties as if he had nothing to do with them.

Closely connected with his ability to analyze but properly considered another quality—because so many intelligent people lack it—was his ability to conclude, to decide. Of all his attributes, this was the best known. Truman's businesslike procedures were a breath of fresh air to General Marshall, who had often dealt with President Roosevelt. Marshall disliked the tortuous nature of Roosevelt's decision making, FDR's tendency to agree with the last man to whom he talked, his habit of giving in to propositions of flashy people who caught his attention and captivated him with talk. Marshall believed that Roosevelt often looked for short-cuts and had an eye out for political sides of problems. One had to watch him and, if possible, follow the stratagem of Secretary of Labor Perkins, who had known Roosevelt when he was a small-time politician in New York state, years before. Miss Perkins always made a memorandum of the conversation after she had obtained a decision from Roosevelt, and she sent a copy to the president for his files, to cover herself in case he tried to change his mind. Roosevelt seemed always to be intriguing for some unknown purpose. Marshall always refused to go when he was invited up to Hyde Park for a few days, in fear that Roosevelt would push him into agreement on some project. The only time he went to Hyde Park was for FDR's funeral.

Contrary to public impression, Truman's decisiveness did not involve haste, and if necessary he refused to make a decision. A classic example was his behavior during the Berlin blockade in 1948, when the Russians closed the borders of the city to land traffic and the only way to supply it was by air. In the early summer, after the barriers went up, Truman's advisers subjected him to tremendous pressure. From one side—General Lucius D. Clay in Berlin and Averell Harriman, the wartime ambassador to Russia—came stentorian argument that the United States "stay in Berlin," come what may, and if necessary send an armored convoy down the Autobahn from Helmstedt, the nearest point of American-governed territory. From the other side—Secretary of the Army Royall and General Bradley—came the argument that Berlin, deep in the Soviet zone of Germany, was unmanageable, too remote from bases; hence, the quicker the United States got out with a bow and scrape to the freedom of the people of West Berlin, the better for everyone. Both sides within the American government beseeched Truman to make up his mind. From the man who "loved to make decisions," however—the president whose "initial impulse when an issue came before him was to make a firm decision then and there"— came no decision. At one point, according to the diary of Secretary of Defense Forrestal, Truman said, "We are going to stay, period." However, later that same day, he said that his decision was "tentative" and that he would make "no black or white decision now." He told Royall, one of the would-be movers and shakers, that he would deal with the situation as it developed. In short, Truman temporized. Eventually, the airlift, begun the day after the blockade, made a decision to stay or leave unnecessary.

In addition to decisiveness when needed, analytical ability, and modesty, a fourth quality of the president was conspicuous willingness, indeed eagerness, to work hard. Without this last quality, Truman would have accomplished little in the presidency and never would have risen to his high office in the first place. Ability to work hard is the very quality of greatness; with few exceptions, the leaders of men in this world have been indefatigable workers, and Harry S. Truman was one of the great company of overachievers. Truman learned to work hard on the farm and ever afterward arose at early hours—4:00 or 5:00 A.M.—regardless of when he went to bed. He often was at his White House desk long before breakfast, reading the Bible, signing mail, writing longhand letters to friends and relatives, or writing diary entries or memoranda of what was on his mind. He also did a tremendous amount of reading, which was not always easy for him because his eyes would smart from too much fine print. He liked to say he had been "fine printed" many times, but he seldom complained about the stacks of memos and other documents that came his way for comment or information or because of confusion or a feeling that the president "should see this." The reading began early in the morning, and it went on late into the night, for Truman always took a full briefcase of material to read in the private White House apartments. By the latter years of his presidency, television was coming in, and the president sometimes watched prizefights and quiz shows, but usually he did not bother and spent his leisure time with paperwork. He had to go to many dinners, receptions, and meetings, but he tried to get back early, and he liked to go to bed at 9:00, which made it easier to get up at 4:00 or 5:00 A.M.

When it came to seeing people in the office, Truman was equally industrious. As his secretaries scheduled appointments, he saw people, careful to hear their problems and if necessary solve them, and moved to the next visitor. He kept the line going diplomatically, only occasionally running behind, as for example, when a congressman in a wheelchair came in and talked for forty-five minutes in favor of a nominee for a federal judgeship about whom the president had already made up his mind. Truman sat quietly and gave the appearance of attention until the congressman ran out of words. After an aide wheeled the visitor out, the president tried to repair his schedule without annoying the individuals who, so proud of their appointments, sat waiting their turns. Truman saw dozens of people each day, dealing with every one of them attentively; he kept his temper and behaved graciously in their presence and in this manner took care of the nation's business.

In formal group meetings, Truman managed his participation with indefatigable dispatch. He measured his time carefully, and, if he had to make remarks or speeches, he put as much time into their preparation as he could. Public commentaries were a problem, for by the time he became president he could not possibly have personally written everything he had to say. If he was speaking to small groups, he read whatever his aides put in front of him, leafing through it first for a feeling of the prose and to see if, by chance, something untoward might be included. For longer and more important speeches, especially when the press might quote him, the president took the drafts and made them his own by interpolations. Sometimes he wrote a draft to compare with the remarks drawn up by his aides. Beginning in the early summer of 1948, he took chances with extemporaneous speeches, for he had become increasingly sensitive to his awkwardness in reading a text. The procedure proved effective, far more so than he had imagined, and he used it on campaign trips that summer and autumn. It was, of course, another charge on his energies, for every speech became an occasion when he not only had to watch for the circumstances of the moment but also had to think out what he was saying and do it fast enough so as not to fumble for words and lose his audience.

Truman's sheer physical ability to work hard was the more remarkable because of his age; he was almost sixty-one in April 1945 when he took office, and when he left the presidency in January 1953, he was sixty-eight—an age by which most people have slowed down considerably. He did not slow down after the presidency, either, but continued to turn out letters, make trips, give speeches, and write books, until he suffered the fall in the bathroom of the Independence house, at the age of eighty. He failed physically thereafter, although he held on to life for another eight years.

"Hot Piano," by Ben Shahn

The Contemporary Misjudgment

HISTORICAL JUDGMENT cannot be hasty, but surely Harry S. Truman will go down in history as one of the best American presidents. The judgment of seventy-five prominent historians in 1962 will stand: they put Truman in the category of "near-great," just after Lincoln, Washington, Franklin D. Roosevelt, Wilson, and Jefferson, all of whom were "great," followed by Jackson, Theodore Roosevelt, James K. Polk, and Truman, who, together with John Adams and Grover Cleveland, were "near-great." Polls taken in 1981 and 1982 advanced Truman's standing from ninth to eighth, ahead of Polk. The question that confronts the student of history, however, is why Truman's contemporaries so often underestimated him.

Not all of his contemporaries thought poorly of Truman. In 1952, for example, he entertained Winston Churchill aboard the *Williamsburg* (by this time Churchill was back in office as prime minister). After dinner, the president's guest seemed to doze off, his chin dropping against his chest, an empty whiskey and soda glass at his elbow, his long black cigar unlit and cradled in the V of his two fingers. Then the old statesman raised his eyelids and gazed at the president. "The last time you and I sat across the conference table was at Potsdam, Mr. President," he said. Grinning, Truman nodded. Churchill continued: "I must confess, sir, I held you in a very low regard then. I loathed your taking the place of Franklin Roosevelt." Truman's grin vanished.

"I misjudged you badly," said Churchill. "Since that time, you, more than any other man, have saved Western civilization.

When the British could no longer hold out in Greece, you, and you alone, sir, made the decision that saved that ancient land from the Communists. You acted in similar fashion . . . when the Soviets tried to take over Iran. Then there was your resolute stand on Trieste, and your Marshall Plan which rescued Western Europe wallowing in the shallows and indeed easy prey to Joseph Stalin's malevolent intentions. Then you established the North Atlantic Treaty Alliance and collective security for those nations against the military machinations of the Soviet Union. Then there was your audacious Berlin Airlift. And, of course, there was Korea." Truman's grin returned.

For the most part, however, there was contemporary misjudgment of Truman, and, years after his death, it is possible to see several reasons for it. The first was his disconcerting way of being himself; if he seemed momentarily to stand on the rim of greatness, he delighted in shattering the illusion by doing something ordinary, such as playing the piano in public. Jokes about him got back to him and he repeated them—even originating one of them, about having played the piano in a bawdy house. Sometimes one error would lead to another, as when, early in 1945, the actress Lauren Bacall crawled on top of an upright piano at which the then vice-president sat and photographers had a field day, even though Truman tried to look the other way. Truman had nothing to do with this publicity stunt—Miss Bacall's agent had virtually shoved her up on top of the piano—but if he had not been playing the piano, it would not have happened. He also carelessly or intentionally subtracted from his dignity at times with salty language. This aspect of his personality was widely known; years later, a story made the rounds that, after the birth of his first grandchild, Truman told his daughter Margaret, "When he gets older, I'm going to teach him to talk." "The hell you are!" Margaret was supposed to have replied. The president enjoyed the barnyard humor of his old army friend, Harry Vaughan, the major general with the double chin, the gaudy rows of campaign ribbons, and the laughing comment, "I'm still with ya, Boss!"

When afflicted with seasickness during a presidential yacht trip, Vaughan was irrepressible: "But what the hell," whooped the general, "it tastes just as good coming up as it did going down."

All the president's known likes and dislikes confirmed the impression given by his rendition of Paderewski's "Minuet in G," his casual speech, and his jokes and jokers. He described modern painting as "ham-and-egg art" ("the kind where you throw an egg at the canvas and then smear it with ham"). He liked ordinary food (ham or roast beef sandwiches for lunch, roast beef and potatoes and custard pie or watermelon for supper). Critics commented on his poker games, known to intimates as "studies in probabilities." He was conservative on women's rights ("a lot of hooey," he once observed), and, when he was asked what he thought of the chances of a woman being president, he replied, "I've said for a long time that women have everything else, they might as well have the presidency."

The president met fire with fire, whatever offense to his dignity might result. One evening, back home in Independence, he summoned a group of male friends known as the Harpie Club to enjoy a pleasant evening of poker, only to discover the next morning that the story was all over the Kansas City *Star* and presumably by that time had been picked up by the wire services. He believed this was an invasion of his privacy, and he was furious—although he was unaware that the *Star*'s inoffensive reporter, Fred Schulenberg, had simply stationed himself outside the iron gate in front of the house, had seen the fellows go inside, and had learned from children who went in for autographs that poker chips and cards were around. That morning, the president went into the grocery store of his old army friend, the mayor of Independence, Roger Sermon, called in a *Star* reporter, and gave him complete information on what he, Truman, had done that morning up to that time. He spared nothing.

Americans also underestimated him because of their own confusion about the reform of government, the change from a small officialdom with limited purposes to a bureaucracy of social salvation. This movement had gone through several incarnations, from progressivism in the time of Theodore Roosevelt to FDR's New Deal and Truman's Fair Deal. The new role of government became to protect the citizenry from unfair actions by their fellows and to redistribute the national wealth and give the underprivileged a chance. In the late 1940s and early 1950s, there was some feeling that Franklin Roosevelt had been a traitor to his class and that there was a need to roll back the legislation of the New Deal. People who had gotten their start through the Roosevelt revolution had come along far enough that they thought they were on their own, and they disliked policies that they believed were financed with their hard-earned money. Memory of the Great Depression was disappearing from 1945 to 1953, and talk of communism abroad led to talk of communism at home. The old idea revived that the American economy was a zero-sum game, wherein anything put in one pocket had to come from another, and this confusion of logic with economics focused on the president of the United States.

Truman won in 1948 not because of his feistiness but because he was the nominee of the party of FDR and the New Deal. There was consensus on the value of the New Deal. Many people hated the New Deal, however, and turned their dislike into irritation with everything Truman stood for in domestic politics.

A third reason his contemporaries underestimated Truman was the foreign policy that he began at the beginning of his presidency, in the year of decisions, and brought into heroic achievement in 1947–1949 with the Truman Doctrine, the Marshall Plan, and NATO, an achievement confirmed by the similarly successful Berlin airlift and Korean War. Truman forthrightly described what was happening and what was necessary. It was not an attractive change, and many Americans sought some single person to blame for their new responsibilities abroad. Harry S. Truman focused their unease, their discontent.

The years went by, and by the time he died, on December 26, 1972, much of the tumult of Truman's era had passed. His daughter Margaret's biography of her father, published in 1973, became a best-seller. So did Merle Miller's *Plain Speaking: An Oral Biography of Harry S. Truman*, published the next year. Samuel Gallu's stage play, *Give 'em Hell, Harry!* starring James Whitmore, opened in 1975 and became a box-office hit. Two or three television dramatizations presented highly favorable accounts of Truman—a marked contrast to a decade earlier, when Truman himself had made a series of television programs that were offered for sale commercially, and stations refused to buy them. Surely the Watergate debacle had effect here: the man of Independence seemed such a contrast to President Nixon. Bumper stickers appeared with the legend, "America needs you, Harry Truman."

Even Republicans took over the memory of this distinctly Democratic president. Senator Barry Goldwater said that Truman was his favorite twentieth-century president. President Gerald R. Ford hung a portrait of Truman in the cabinet room and placed a bust of Truman near his desk in the Oval Office. Ford's successor, Jimmy Carter, continued the adulation, putting Truman's sign, "The Buck Stops Here," atop his desk.

Meanwhile, in 1975, the rock group "Chicago" had recorded a new hit entitled "Harry Truman," and *Time* magazine published an article about the phenomenon of Truman's popularity, entitled "Trumania." The number of visitors to the Harry S. Truman Library and Museum in Independence increased dramatically; carloads of tourists from all over the United States and buses full of senior citizens and junior citizens filled the half-circle road in front of the building bumper-to-bumper, and the lobby swarmed with people buying postcards and "The Buck Stops Here" signs and phonograph records and plaster busts of Harry Truman.

The judgment of Truman's historical greatness is now almost certain. His personal awkwardnesses, if such they were, have been swept away, forgotten by the aging adults of Truman's time and unknown to young adults of the 1980s. The main lines of this century's social and economic revolution have held, as have the lines of foreign policy—Truman's creation that preserved the Republic into our own time.

A Note on the Sources

CHRONICLING THE LIFE of a great public figure of recent times can be a very uncertain enterprise for a biographer. Surmise and speculation make the rounds, appear in articles and books, and, through sheer repetition, take on a life of their own. It is difficult to know what, then, really happened in the life of the public figure, to separate fact from surmise. In the case of Harry S. Truman, fortunately, the availability of an extraordinary collection of private papers at the Harry S. Truman Library in Independence, Missouri—beginning in the mid-1970s, shortly after Truman's death, and ending in 1980, when the archivists analyzed and readied the last boxes—has put major resources at the disposal of the biographer, and these sources are the foundation of this book.

The Truman papers that became available in the latter 1970s were weak in their coverage of the president's early years. Unlike Mrs. James Roosevelt—who, when her son Franklin Delano was born in 1882, was seized at once by a certainty that he would rise to renown, therefore saving everything he wrote—Mrs. John A. Truman had no such hallucination in 1884 and would have laughed in the face of anyone who might have come down the country road to Lamar and said that Harry S. Truman would become president of the United States. "Shucks!" Mrs. Truman would have said, or "Pshaw!" or "Fiddle-sticks!" For that reason, and perhaps also because of the cost of paper in those days—which would not have bothered the Hyde Park Roosevelts but would have bothered the Lamar Trumans, for whom it was still the time of slates—no composition by Harry S. Truman seems to have survived from the years of his life until graduation from high school. At Hyde Park, young Roosevelt had had two tutors, and his mother had stored away his childhood compositions for posterity, but nothing of Truman's apparently survived the moths and rust of his time.

The first extant Truman letter is a piece of typewriting—a half-sheet
sent from Spalding's Commercial College in Kansas City on July 1,
1901, to Grandmother Young, Uncle Harrison, and Harrison's sister,
Laura Jane Young Everhart—in which the typist set out his holiday
plans: "The fourth will be here soon and, as I get a few days holiday
James Wright, the boy who was out there with me once before, and I
are comming out to celebrate. We will be there Wednesday for supper if
nothing happens. We shall bring our fire-works along with us and
celebrate out there if you have no objection. As Mary wrote to you
yesterday I wont ware your patience out by saying too much. Please
excuse the mistakes as this is my first letter on the type-writer. Hoping
you can read this and that it will find you all well I close with love to all
as Yours truly Harry Truman."

The next known Truman manuscript is three sheets on the stationery
of the National Bank of Commerce in Kansas City, sent to Ethel and
Nellie Noland on February 2, 1904, by "Horatio," as his cousins called
him. At the top of the stationery appears the legend, "Capital
$1,000,000.00." and Horatio playfully wrote a "My" to the left of
"Capital." Down below he explained: "The naughts are on the wrong
side." The letter made an arrangement for Ethel and Nellie to come
into the city: "I'll meet you at EBT & Co's Walnut st entrance on Sat.
Feb 6'04 at 2:15 P.M. and will have *him* along if possible (That's for
Nellie.) If not he'll come to the theater *Later*. I shall expect you all to go
home with me and stay till Sunday any way if you can do so write me at
home 2108 Park. I think if you will go home with me to supper Mr H
will too [Mr. Henderson also worked at the Commerce]. I understand
that Mr Beresford is exceedingly good so don't fail to come. I've *all
ready* got the seats so if you fail I'll have to take some hobos and I don't
want to do that. Write immediately if you'll stay till Sunday to."

For the years on the farm, 1906 to 1917, there is not much other than
a few letters to the Noland sisters and one long letter to Judge Allen C.
Southern of Independence, dated August 3, 1915. The letter is on the
stationery of "J. A. Truman & Son, Farmers, Kansas City Home
Phone—Hickman 6." Judge Southern had sent out questions and
answers about payments for teams and men doing township road work,
and Truman, as a road overseer, did not care for them: "With all due
respect to you and the Senator, it seems to me that you have a little too
much law and not much common sense mixed in these questions and
answers."

Truman's two years in the army inspired postcards and a half-dozen or so letters to Cousin Ethel, but they were subject to censorship and contain little of historical value.

His period on the county court in the 1920s and early 1930s yielded very little material of a personal sort. The official correspondence for that period has disappeared. Beginning in 1931, however, Truman stayed overnight several times in the Pickwick Hotel, a hostelry in Kansas City now used as a nursing home, and each time he took up hotel stationery to write out his ideas of the moment. Some accounts dealt with army life, but most concerned personalities on the county court. These writings are extremely frank; they run to several dozen pages and are worth close attention. William D. Tammeus published excerpts in the Kansas City *Star* in October 1980.

Beginning in 1935, when Truman went to the Senate, there must have been a bulky correspondence, but little survived, for during World War II his staff sent the papers to storage and they disappeared, probably being thrown away. What materials survived are formal, papers that Truman had looked over in committee assignments. What a biographer likes, however, is official correspondence of a sharply interesting sort. Apparently few family letters from this important time in Truman's life have survived. One must assume that he wrote to his sister Mary Jane and to his mother, since the 1930s and early 1940s were an era when long-distance telephone calls were a luxury, and Truman was accustomed to write to them even when he was president. Regarding letters to Bess Truman, Margaret Truman has related that the president came into the living room of the Independence house one day and found his wife burning his letters. He told her that she shouldn't do that. Bess said that she had read them several times and did not need to do so again. "But think of history," said the president. "I have," was her answer.

Some few letters from the senatorial and vice presidential periods have survived in the papers of Truman's cousins, the Noland sisters, and those of his cousin Major General Ralph Truman, with whom he was close.

The president possessed an acute feeling for history, and he was aware that very few personal papers had survived to document his life until he entered the presidency at the age of sixty. He wrote out several autobiographical accounts. The first, already mentioned, were in the Hotel Pickwick papers; many of these were ruminatingly autobiographical. The second account was a single-spaced, 12,000-word, handwritten account of his life from graduation from high school in 1901 until early in 1945, when the then vice-president took his pen in hand and wrote it out. A third autobiographical accounting came in late 1951 or early 1952, when the president brought into his office on several mornings big sheaves of handwritten reminiscences, about 8,000 words, which partly duplicated the memoir of early 1945 but included a long narrative of his early years, beginning with his first memory—chasing a frog around the backyard of a farmhouse when he was two years old in 1886. These several narrative accounts of his life until his presidency show a remarkable agreement in particulars— friends and acquaintances always maintained that Truman had an excellent memory. They fit together well into a narrative, and I have published them as *The Autobiography of Harry S. Truman* (Boulder: Colorado Associated University Press, 1980).

When he became president, Truman had no more problems with office staff, and his dictation was done in one or more copies that were duly filed. A massive set of papers was put together gradually; most of it went to the Truman Library after the president's departure from Washington in 1953. The Central Files of the Truman administration are huge—2,700 feet of materials. What made the work of historians of the Truman administration extremely difficult until the president's private papers were made available in the 1970s, however, was the fact that the Central Files were often quite dull. A reader could pull out a valuable nugget here and there, but he had to look almost endlessly.

The best of the president's papers were not in the central files but in about sixty steel cases in Truman's private part of the library, where they remained until after his death, when Margaret Truman, as his executor, released them to the library and the archivists put them in archival boxes and opened them to scholars. These papers were under the president's control until his death, and he refused to allow anyone to look at them except his daughter, who was working on a biography. When asked by scholars for access to these private papers, the president sometimes refused angrily, as when the newspaperman Cabell Phillips journeyed to Independence on what he supposed was an invitation from the president to see everything, only to discover that this did not mean *everything*. When the papers were made available, they proved exciting. The president's private secretary, Rose Conway, had kept these files, and the materials for the presidential years were known as the President's Secretary's Files (PSF). Miss Conway kept everything, with almost no exceptions (a hot letter to Henry Wallace asking for his resignation never found its way into the files), and these letters, little handwritten presidential memoranda, and hasty diary entries about whatever came to the president's mind are now in the PSF, which has 339 boxes—113 feet of material. The material is dated by groups of boxes, with a short breakdown for individual boxes.

In the materials that were opened beginning in about 1975 were also the Post-Presidential Files (PPF), nearly a thousand boxes, including correspondence through the years after Truman's departure from the White House. The PPF has three runs of correspondence, with material filed roughly according to the importance of the correspondent. The largest run, several hundred boxes, is the General File, almost entirely routine and of interest only for the occasional annotations in the president's handwriting ("File and forget." "File it. No ans. I told him the facts and he has garbled them." "File it. The old man will write us every day if this is answered." "F & F" "Thank him & tell him the Louisville Courier-Journal has always been after circulation and not facts & morals." "File it. No interest. The figure is 100% wrong but as Coolidge said don't argue with skunks.") The other runs are more interesting. The middle-sized run, the Name File, has ninety-five boxes; the smallest, the Secretary's Office File, has thirty-five. An interesting group in the PPF is the Desk File, which has three boxes containing material found in President Truman's desk at the time of his death; his desk was a rat's nest of correspondence, casual diary entries, and memos that Miss Conway never got her hands on, and the contents are sometimes fascinating. In the nature of all filing systems, the PPF like the PSF tended to get out of order as the years passed, and it is necessary to follow the calendar carefully, frequently searching out materials with a sort of historical carpet sweeper, taking chances of looking through uninviting boxes.

The Truman Library has sought to gather the personal papers of cabinet officials, White House assistants, and other officers of the Truman administration, and many of these are now in the library and available to researchers. In the collections of personal papers are such gems as the letter that former Undersecretary of State Webb wrote former Secretary of the Treasury Snyder in 1975 on the twenty-fifth anniversary of the Korean War, in which Webb recalled the opening days of the war. Charles G. Ross kept a diary for part of 1946. There is

also the detailed diary of Eben A. Ayers, who, as assistant press
secretary in 1945–1950, attended the morning conferences of the
president and his immediate office assistants and later helped the
president draw together his personal papers for shipment to Independence. Lawrence A. Yates is preparing the Ayers diary for publication by
the University of Missouri Press.

The Truman Library possesses excellent oral history interviews,
which have been typed double-spaced and sometimes run to several
hundred pages. The best of them is an interview with the State
Department official Loy W. Henderson by Richard D. McKinzie on
June 14 and July 5, 1973. This interview is excellent because the
interviewer knew what to ask; it is especially good on Palestine and
Iran and generally good on the State Department. Most of the oral
history interviews are available on interlibrary loan.

Documentary materials on the Truman era are numerous. The most
important are the annual volumes of *Public Papers of Harry S. Truman*
(Washington, D.C.: Government Printing Office, 1961ff), which include
all the speeches and press conferences; and *Harry S. Truman, Late a
President of the United States: Memorial Tributes Delivered in Congress*
(Washington, D.C.: Government Printing Office, 1973), which contains
many remarkable testimonies.

Some privately collected documentary accounts of Truman and his
times are William Hillman, *Mr. President* (New York: Farrar, Straus and
Young, 1952), an authorized publication of diary entries, interviews,
and the third Truman autobiographical account, written especially for
that book; Barton J. Bernstein and Allen J. Matusow, eds., *The Truman
Administration: A Documentary History* (New York: Harper and Row, 1966);
and Herbert Druks, *From Truman through Johnson: A Documentary History*,
vol. 1, *Truman and Eisenhower* (New York: Robert Speller, 1971).

The Truman Library has sponsored conferences of scholars and
former leading officials of the Truman administration, and the results
of several meetings have appeared in mimeographed or book form. For
one of the earlier sessions, see Robert H. Ferrell and Jerry N. Hess,
eds., *Conference of Scholars on the European Recovery Program, March 20–21,
1964* (Independence: Harry S. Truman Library Institute, 1964). For the
later books, edited by Francis H. Heller, see below.

Researchers on the Truman years should consult the two books
edited by Richard S. Kirkendall, both entitled *The Truman Period as a
Research Field*, the first published in 1967 (Columbia: University of

Missouri Press), the second in 1974. The second book, subtitled *A Reappraisal, 1972*, set out the new literature of the late 1960s and early 1970s.

Mention has been made of *The Autobiography of Harry S. Truman*. The reader may also wish to consult my *Off the Record: The Private Papers of Harry S. Truman* (New York: Harper & Row, 1980), a selection of diary entries, memoranda, and letters in the PSF and PPF, from 1945 to 1971.

In the mid-1950s, President Truman published his memoirs in two volumes, *Year of Decisions* (Garden City, N.Y.: Doubleday, 1955) and *Years of Trial and Hope* (1956). The volumes are unfortunately divided, with a single year's events related in the first volume and the remaining seven years of the presidency in the second. Almost as an afterthought, Truman placed a short account of his life from birth to the White House in the middle of the initial volume, pp. 112–198, allotting it only a little more space than the Potsdam Conference (pp. 332–414).

The problem with the Truman memoirs was twofold. When Truman returned to Independence, he failed to obtain the services of a first-rate literary assistant and entrusted the work to several well-meaning, intelligent, but unskilled aides, who piled up prose in a disorderly way until they lost control of the literary heap. The evidence in the Memoirs File of the PPF shows that the president did his best to cooperate and spent interminable hours making dozens of useless tapes in response to inept questions. As a result, the assistants expanded their materials into enormously detailed drafts and lost control. His publisher, Doubleday, dispatched a professional writer, Ernest Havemann, but he was not able to help much. Fortunately, Francis Heller of the University of Kansas, a clear thinker, came into the project and brought order out of the chaos before Doubleday's date for receipt of the manuscript. There was also another problem in writing the memoirs; the president's assistants were so far from recognizing good prose that they cut and chopped Truman's nicely written commentaries and descriptions until they did not sound at all like their intelligent author.

In retirement, the president produced two books in addition to his memoirs. The first was *Mr. Citizen* (New York: Geis Associates, 1960), essays about the problem of readjustment after leaving the White House. On January 20, 1953, as the limousine was taking the Trumans from President Eisenhower's inaugural ceremony across Washingtown to Georgetown to the luncheon with former Secretary Acheson and other officials, Margaret Truman turned to her father and said, "Hello,

Mister Truman," providing the theme of this book. In 1959, Truman spoke to undergraduates at Columbia, and the lectures and ensuing questions are in *Truman Speaks* (New York: Columbia University Press, 1960).

Margaret Truman published *Souvenir: Margaret Truman's Own Story*, with Margaret Cousins (New York: McGraw-Hill, 1956), a delightful volume about growing up in Missouri and Washington when one's father is successively senator, vice-president, and president. Margaret has also edited *Letters from Father: The Truman Family's Personal Correspondence* (New York: Arbor House, 1981), covering the time when her father's absences from Washington or Independence made letters necessary. Margaret admits that she was a terrible correspondent and that the letters were less frequent than they might have been. Other letters in the book are from her mother, from Grandmother Wallace, from Mrs. George P. (Aunt Beuf) Wallace, and from miscellaneous other relatives.

The best single-volume biography of Truman is also by Margaret Truman: *Harry S. Truman* (New York: William Morrow, 1973) is an able book that is in part reminiscence but in larger part an analysis of what made Truman a success in the presidency. It is favorable to its subject, but the point of view is convincing, and it is nicely written, at times exhilarating in its drawing of the emotion that surrounded the president's successes and occasional failures. It also deals at length with Truman's early years.

Also important for an understanding of Truman's early life is Jonathan Daniels, *The Man of Independence* (Philadelphia: J. B. Lippincott, 1950), written with Truman's assistance to correct surmise and speculation about his life. Its author went to Independence and environs and spoke to many of the president's contemporaries, even to members of the older generation, and of course to the relatives. Not long afterward, the individuals to whom he applied for information about the almost-forgotten years prior to the county judge era began to die, and many were gone before the oral history program of the Truman Library got to them.

The two-volume presidential biography by Robert J. Donovan, *Conflict and Crisis: The Presidency of Harry S. Truman, 1945–1948* (New York: W. W. Norton, 1977) and *Tumultuous Years: . . . 1949–1953* (1982) is definitive. Donovan was a reporter for the *Herald Tribune* during the Truman years and is an indefatigable researcher.

Of the one-volume biographies, the two best, other than Margaret Truman's book, are Cabell Phillips, *The Truman Presidency: The History of a Triumphant Succession* (New York: Macmillan, 1966), and Alfred Steinberg, *The Man from Missouri: The Life and Times of Harry S. Truman* (New York: Putnam, 1962). Phillips was a *New York Times* reporter in Washington during the Truman years, and he writes with sure feeling for the era; his judgments are acute and his book is very well written. Steinberg also has a good sense of the times and writes well. See also Frank McNaughton and Walter Hehmeyer, *Harry Truman: President* (New York: Whittlesea House, 1948); Bert Cochran, *Harry Truman and the Crisis Presidency* (New York: Funk and Wagnalls, 1973); and especially Francis Heller, "Truman," in Lord Longford and Sir John Wheeler Bennett, eds., *The History Makers* (London: Sidgwick and Jackson, 1973), pp. 322–335. It is also worthwhile looking at Robert S. Allen and William V. Shannon, *The Truman Merry-Go-Round* (New York: Vanguard, 1950), a racy, gossipy, critical book. If the authors found a few intelligent men around Truman, they hesitated to admit it; as Gerald W. Johnson and Samuel Lubell wrote: if the administration was so bad, then how did the United States of America survive until the book's publication? After Truman died, there was a rush into print, notably by Merle Miller, *Plain Speaking: An Oral Biography of Harry S. Truman* (New York: Berkley, 1974), a book that rested on an unsubstantiated body of material, including interviews. Some Miller items are believable and others doubtful, especially the president's language, although the book is wonderful reading. Samuel Gallu's play of 1975, *Give 'em Hell, Harry!* contains commentaries from books and newspaper accounts; it was also converted into a movie. John Lukacs, *1945 Year Zero* (Garden City, N.Y.: Doubleday, 1978) has a fine essay on Truman. Charles Robbins and Bradley Smith, *Last of His Kind: An Informal Portrait of Harry S. Truman* (New York: William Morrow, 1979) offers the experience of author Robbins who, with photographer Smith, interviewed Truman in 1953 in Independence for five articles published in *The American Weekly* under the title "Mr. Citizen." Robbins went back in 1977 and wrote of the presidential image after a quarter-century. Smith's unposed black-and-white photos of Truman immediately after he left the presidency, taken in Independence and during an automobile trip to Washington that summer, look as if they were made yesterday. Harold F. Gosnell, *Truman's Crises: A Political Biography of Harry S. Truman* (Westport, Conn.: Greenwood, 1980) reflects research of the 1960s and makes no use of the PSF and PPF. John Hersey did a profile of Truman for the *New Yorker* in 1950 and republished it, with another profile of President Gerald R. Ford, as *Aspects of the Presidency* (New Haven and New York: Ticknor and Fields, 1980). Hersey saw much of President Truman for a few weeks in 1950, and his profile is a stunningly successful description of the man and his times. Robert Underhill, *The Truman Persuasions* (Ames: Iowa State University Press, 1981), is a study of the president's speechmaking but also contains much information from the Truman Library and from wide reading. Monte M. Poen, ed., *Strictly Personal and Confidential: The Unmailed Letters of Harry Truman* (Boston: Little, Brown, 1982), offers nearly 150 letters and memos Truman wrote and had second thoughts about mailing. This wonderful collection is, as Poen's publisher advertises it, "short, pithy, and to the point, full of Harry Truman's sense of fun, salty good humor, and not inconsiderable vitriol."

Readers desiring to learn about Truman's life beyond the manuscripts, documentary collections, presidential memoirs, and biographies, will readily find dozens of books. Only a few touch Truman's early years, such as Lyle W. Dorsett, *The Pendergast Machine* (New York: Oxford University Press, 1968) and Donald H. Riddle, *The Truman Committee* (New Brunswick, N.J.: Rutgers University Press, 1964). Eugene F. Schmidtlein, "Truman the Senator," is an unpublished doctoral dissertation at the University of Missouri. Edward L. Schapsmeier and Frederick H. Schapsmeier, *Prophet in Politics: Henry A. Wallace and the War Years, 1940–1965* (Ames: Iowa State University Press, 1970) considers Senator Truman's rival at the Democratic national convention in 1944, subsequently his secretary of commerce.

Beginning in 1945 with the presidency the books dealing with domestic politics and international affairs are indeed plentiful. General accounts are Eric F. Goldman, *The Crucial Decade* (New York: Knopf, 1956); Herbert Agar, *The Price of Power: America since 1945* (Chicago: University of Chicago Press, 1957); Herbert Druks, *Harry S. Truman and the Russians: 1945–1953* (New York: Speller, 1966); Barton J. Bernstein, ed., *Politics and Policies of the Truman Administration* (Chicago: Quadrangle, 1970); Herbert Feis, *From Trust to Terror: The Onset of the Cold War* (New York: Norton, 1970); Joyce and Gabriel Kolko, *The Limits of Power: The World and United States Foreign Policy, 1945–54* (New York: Harper and

Row (1972); Lawrence S. Kaplan, ed., *Recent American Foreign Policy: Conflicting Interpretations* (rev. ed., Homewood, Ill.: Dorsey Press, 1972); John Lewis Gaddis, *The United States and the Origins of the Cold War, 1941– 1947* (New York: Columbia University Press, 1972); by the same author, *Strategies of Containment: A Critical Appraisal of Postwar American National Security Policy* (New York: Oxford University Press, 1982); Charles Gati, ed., *Caging the Bear: Containment and the Cold War* (Indianapolis: Bobbs-Merrill, 1972); Robert H. Ferrell, ed., *America in a Divided World: 1945– 1972* (New York: Harper and Row, 1975); Walter La Feber, *America, Russia, and the Cold War: 1945–1975* (New York: John Wiley, 1976); Thomas H. Etzold and John Lewis Gaddis, eds., *Containment: Documents on American Policy and Strategy, 1945–1950* (New York: Columbia University Press, 1978); Daniel Yergin, *Shattered Peace: The Origins of the Cold War and the National Security State* (Boston: Houghton Mifflin, 1978); Oscar Handlin, *The Distortion of America* (Boston: Little, Brown, 1981).

For the "year of decisions" see Athan G. Theoharis, *The Yalta Myths: An Issue in U.S. Politics, 1945–1955* (Columbia: University of Missouri Press, 1970); Lisle A. Rose, *After Yalta: America and the Origins of the Cold War* (New York: Charles Scribner's Sons, 1973); Rose's *Dubious Victory: The United States and the End of World War II* (Kent, Ohio: Kent State University Press, 1973); Herbert Feis, *Between War and Peace: The Potsdam Conference* (Princeton: Princeton University Press, 1960): Thomas G. Paterson, *Soviet-American Confrontation: Postwar Reconstruction and the Origins of the Cold War* (Baltimore: Johns Hopkins University Press, 1973); Paterson's *On Every Front: The Making of the Cold War* (New York: Norton, 1979); Robert M. Hathaway, *Ambiguous Partnership: Britain and America, 1944–1947* (New York: Columbia University Press, 1981); Terry H. Anderson, *The United States, Great Britain, and the Cold War, 1944–1947* (Columbia: University of Missouri Press, 1981). The decision to use the atomic bomb appears in Louis Morton's chapter of the same name, in Kent Roberts Greenfield, ed., *Command Decisions* (Washington: Government Printing Office, 1960); Herbert Feis, *The Atomic Bomb and the End of World War II* (Princeton: Princeton University Press, 1960); Richard G. Hewlett and Oscar E. Anderson, Jr., *The New World: 1939– 1946* (University Park, Penn.: Pennsylvania State University Press, 1962); Hewlett and Francis Duncan, *Atomic Shield: 1947–1952* (University Park, Penn.: Pennsylvania State University Press, 1969); *The Journals of David E. Lilienthal* (New York: Harper and Row, 1964–); Alice Kimball Smith, *A Peril and a Hope: The Scientists' Movement in America, 1945–47* (Chicago: University of Chicago Press, 1965); Martin J. Sherwin, *A World Destroyed: The Atomic Bomb and the Grand Alliance* (New York: Knopf, 1975); Michael Mandelbaum, *The Nuclear Question: The United States and Nuclear Weapons, 1946–1976* (New York: Cambridge University Press, 1979); the same author's *The Nuclear Revolution: International Politics before and after Hiroshima* (New York: Cambridge University Press, 1981); Gregg F. Herken, *The Winning Weapon: The Atomic Bomb in the Cold War* (New York: Knopf, 1981); McGeorge Bundy, "The Missed Chance to Stop the H-Bomb," *New York Review of Books*, May 13, 1982. On the German question see Marshall Knappen, *And Call it Peace* (Chicago: University of Chicago Press, 1947); Lucius D. Clay, *Decision in Germany* (Garden City, N.Y.: Doubleday, 1950); Eugene Davidson, *The Death and Life of Germany: An Account of the American Occupation* (New York: Knopf, 1959); the same author's *The Trial of the Germans: An Account of the Twenty-Two Defendants before the International Military Tribunal at Nuremberg* (New York: Macmillan, 1966); and Davidson's *The Nuremberg Fallacy: Wars and War Crimes since World War II* (New York: Macmillan, 1973); Harry L. Coles and Albert K. Weinberg, *Civil Affairs: Soldiers Become Governors* (Washington: Government Printing Office, 1964); John Gimbel, *The American Occupation of Germany* (Stanford, Calif.: Stanford University Press, 1968); Bruce Kuklick, *American Policy and the Division of Germany: The Clash with Russia over Reparations* (Ithaca, N.Y.: Cornell University Press, 1972); David Herschler, "Retreat in Germany: The Decision to Withdraw Anglo-American Forces from the Soviet Occupational Zone, 1945," and Daniel Harrington, "The Berlin Blockade," dissertations at Indiana University, 1977, 1980. Eastern Europe, a subject of much concern in the first postwar years, appears in Stephen D. Kertesz, *Diplomacy in a Whirlpool* (Notre Dame, Ind.: University of Notre Dame Press, 1953); and the same writer's edited book, *The Fate of East Central Europe* (Notre Dame, Ind.: University of Notre Dame Press, 1956).

The change in American foreign relations appears in biographies and memoirs of the secretaries of state: Richard L. Walker and George Curry, *E. R. Stettinius, Jr. and James F. Byrnes* (New York: Cooper Square Publishers, 1965); James F. Byrnes, *Speaking Frankly* (New York: Harper, 1947); Byrnes' *All in One Lifetime* (New York: Harper, 1958); Patricia Dawson Ward, *The Threat of Peace: James F. Byrnes and the Council of Foreign*

Ministers, 1945–1946 (Kent, Ohio: Kent State University Press, 1979); Kendrick A. Clements, ed., *James F. Byrnes and the Origins of the Cold War* (Durham, N.C.: Carolina Academic Press, 1982); Robert L. Messer, *The End of an Alliance: James F. Byrnes, Roosevelt, Truman, and the Origins of the Cold War* (Chapel Hill: University of North Carolina Press, 1982); Robert H. Ferrell, *George C. Marshall* (New York: Cooper Square Publishers, 1966); Dean Acheson, *The Pattern of Responsibility* (Boston: Houghton, Mifflin, 1952); the same author's *Sketches from Life of Men I Have Known* (New York: Harper, 1959); Acheson's *Present at the Creation: My Years in the State Department* (New York: Norton, 1969); Gaddis Smith, *Dean Acheson* (New York: Cooper Square Publishers, 1972); Daniel S. McLellan, *Dean Acheson: The State Department Years* (New York: Dodd, Mead, 1976).

Arthur H. Vandenberg, Jr., ed., *The Private Papers of Senator Vandenberg* (Boston: Houghton, Mifflin, 1952) is the diaries and correspondence of a leading Republican; for Robert A. Taft see James T. Patterson, *Mr. Republican* (Boston: Houghton, Mifflin, 1972); the leader of the House of Representatives, Joe Martin, wrote *My First Fifty Years in Politics* (New York: McGraw-Hill, 1960). On the Democratic side see *My Name is Tom Connally* (New York: Holt, 1954).

Theodore H. White, *Fire in the Ashes: Europe in Mid-Century* (New York: Sloane, 1953) conveys the mood of the Continent in the early postwar years. Truman's speechwriter in the Department of State, Joseph M. Jones, relates *The Fifteen Weeks (February 21–June 5, 1947)* (New York: Viking, 1955); see also Richard M. Freeland, *The Truman Doctrine and the Origins of McCarthyism: Foreign Policy, Domestic Politics, and International Security, 1946–1948* (New York: Knopf, 1972); a much-quoted definition of containment appears in George F. Kennan, "The Sources of Soviet Conduct," *Foreign Affairs*, vol. 25 (1946–1947), 566–582; for the Marshall Plan see Fredrick J. Dobney, ed., *Selected Papers of Will Clayton* (Baltimore: Johns Hopkins University Press, 1971); John Gimbel, *The Origins of the Marshall Plan* (Stanford, Calif.: Stanford University Press, 1976); Susan M. Hartmann, *The Marshall Plan* (Columbus: Charles E. Merrill, 1968). The Middle East appears in Edward H. Buehrig, *The UN and the Palestinian Refugees: A Study in Nonterritorial Administration* (Bloomington: Indiana University Press, 1971); Bruce Kuniholm, *The Origins of the Cold War in the Near East* (Princeton: Princeton University Press, 1979); Allen Weinstein and Moshe Ma'oz, eds., *Truman and the American*

Commitment to Israel (Jerusalem: The Magnes Press of Hebrew University, 1981). A special subject is David Green, *The Containment of Latin America* (Chicago: Quadrangle, 1971).

Dissenters from Truman foreign policy appeared in the late sixties and early seventies, what with the heating up of the Vietnam War, and books of "historical revisionism" appeared that sought to revise the interpretation of the Truman era as a heroic period and indeed to show it as a surrender to imperialism: William A. Williams, *The Tragedy of American Diplomacy* (2d ed., Cleveland: World, 1962); Lloyd C. Gardner, *Architects of Illusion: Men and Ideas in American Foreign Policy, 1941–1949* (Chicago: Quadrangle, 1970); Thomas G. Paterson, ed., *Cold War Critics: Alternatives to American Foreign Policy in the Truman Years* (Chicago: Quadrangle, 1971). Opponents of "revisionism" were Robert W. Tucker, *The Radical Left and American Foreign Policy* (Baltimore: Johns Hopkins University Press, 1971); Joseph M. Siracusa, *New Left Diplomatic Histories and Historians: The American Revisionists* (Port Washington, N.Y.: Kennikat, 1973); Robert James Maddox, *The New Left and the Origins of the Cold War* (Princeton: Princeton University Press, 1973).

Truman's campaign for election in 1948 rested in large part on his ability to continue the New Deal through what he described as the Fair Deal, and the underpinnings of this effort are in Alonzo L. Hamby, *Beyond the New Deal: Harry S. Truman and American Liberalism* (New York: Columbia University Press, 1973). Here the president had to work with Congress, for which see Susan M. Hartmann, *Truman and the 80th Congress* (Columbia: University of Missouri Press, 1971). For separate problems see Richard O. Davies, *Housing Reform during the Truman Administration* (Columbia: University of Missouri Press, 1966); R. Alton Lee, *Truman and Taft-Hartley* (Lexington: University of Kentucky Press, 1966); Arthur F. McClure, *The Truman Administration and the Problems of Postwar Labor: 1945–1948* (Rutherford, N.J.: Fairleigh Dickinson University Press, 1969); Richard Dalfiume, *Desegregation of the Armed Forces: Fighting on Two Fronts, 1939–1953* (Columbia: University of Missouri Press, 1969); William C. Berman, *The Politics of Civil Rights in the Truman Administration* (Columbus: Ohio State University Press, 1970); Donald R. McCoy and Richard T. Ruetten, *Quest and Response: Minority Rights and the Truman Administration* (Lawrence: University Press of Kansas, 1973). The campaign heated up with accusations of scandal, brought together by Jules Abels, *The Truman Scandals* (Chicago: Regnery, 1956). Jack Redding, *Inside the Democratic Party* (Indianapolis: Bobbs-Merrill, 1958) relates the effort to deal with such issues and all the others of 1948, by the Democrats' publicity man. The campaign is in Jules Abels, *Out of the Jaws of Victory* (New York: Holt, 1959); and Irwin Ross, *The Loneliest Campaign: The Truman Victory of 1948* (New York: New American Library, 1968). After the victory came the Brannan Plan, for which see J. Allen Matusow, *Farm Policies and Politics in the Truman Years* (Cambridge, Mass.: Harvard University Press, 1967).

The origins of the Korean War lay in America's Far Eastern policy: Akira Iriye, *The Cold War in Asia* (Englewood Cliffs, N.J.: Prentice-Hall, 1974); Yonosuke Nagai and Akira Iriye, eds., *The Origins of the Cold War in Asia* (New York: Columbia University Press, 1977); Lisle A. Rose, *Roots of Tragedy: The United States and the Struggle for Asia, 1945–1953* (Westport, Conn.: Greenwood Press, 1975). For Japan see William J. Sebald, *With MacArthur in Japan: A Personal History of the Occupation* (New York: Norton, 1965); John M. Allison, *Ambassador from the Prairie or Allison Wonderland* (Boston: Houghton, Mifflin, 1973). China is in Herbert Feis, *The China Tangle* (Princeton: Princeton University Press, 1953); Russell D. Buhite, *Patrick J. Hurley and American Foreign Policy* (Ithaca, N.Y.: Cornell University Press, 1973); Gary May, *China Scapegoat: . . . John Carter Vincent* (Washington: New Republic, 1979); Dorothy Borg and Waldo Heinrichs, *Uncertain Years: Chinese-American Relations, 1947–1950* (New York: Columbia University Press, 1980). Korea, the focus of Far Eastern rivalries, is a complicated subject, for which see Gregory Henderson, *Korea: The Politics of the Vortex* (Cambridge, Mass.: Harvard University Press, 1968); Robert R. Simmons, *The Strained Alliance: Peking, Pyongyang, Moscow, and the Politics of the Korean Civil War* (New York: Free Press, 1975); William W. Stueck, Jr., *The Road to Confrontation* (Chapel Hill: University of North Carolina Press, 1980); Charles M. Dobbs, *The Unwanted Symbol: American Foreign Policy, The Cold War, and Korea, 1945–1950* (Kent, Ohio: Kent State University Press, 1981); Bruce Cumings, *The Origins of the Korean War: Liberation and the Emergence of Separate Regimes, 1945–1947* (Princeton: Princeton University Press, 1981).

Military affairs are set out in detail in the Korean series of the Department of the Army's Center of Military History, published by the Government Printing Office. Matthew B. Ridgway, *The Korean War* (Garden City, N.Y.: Doubleday, 1967) is excellent—authoritative, readable, and short. Richard F. Haynes, *The Awesome Power: Harry S. Truman as Commander in Chief* (Baton Rouge: Louisiana State University Press, 1973) provides the rationale. J. Lawton Collins, *War in Peacetime:*

The History and Lessons of Korea (Boston: Houghton, Mifflin, 1969), by the U.S. Army's chief of staff, is authoritative; for the same author's many years in the military, including the Korean War, see his nostalgic *Lightning Joe: An Autobiography* (Baton Rouge: Louisiana State University Press, 1979). Ronald J. Caridi, *The Korean War and American Politics: The Republican Party as a Case Study* (Philadelphia: University of Pennsylvania Press, 1968) looks at a major aspect of the war. Francis H. Heller, ed., *The Korean War: A 25-Year Perspective* (Lawrence: Regents Press of Kansas, 1977) presents views of leading military and diplomatic officials. For the relief of the Far Eastern commander see Douglas MacArthur, *Reminiscences* (New York: McGraw-Hill, 1964); together with John W. Spanier, *The Truman-MacArthur Controversy and the Korean War* (Cambridge, Mass.: Harvard University Press, 1959); and Richard H. Rovere and Arthur M. Schlesinger, Jr., *The Truman-MacArthur Controversy and American Foreign Policy* (rev. ed., New York: Farrar, Strauss and Giroux, 1965).

The literature of communism includes Alan Moorehead, *The Traitors* (New York: Harper, 1952); Alger Hiss, *In the Court of Public Opinion* (New York: Knopf, 1957); Allen Weinstein, *Perjury: The Hiss-Chambers Case* (New York: Vintage, 1979); Earl Latham, *The Communist Controversy in Washington: From the New Deal to McCarthy* (Cambridge, Mass.: Harvard University Press, 1966); Kim Philby, *My Silent War* (New York: Grove, 1968); Bruce Page, David Leitch, Phillip Knightley, *The Philby Conspiracy* (Garden City, N.Y.: Doubleday, 1968). For the result, McCarthyism, see Richard H. Rovere, *Senator Joe McCarthy* (New York: Harcourt, Brace, 1959); Alan D. Harper, *The Politics of Loyalty: The White House and the Communist Issue, 1946–1952* (Westport, Conn.: Greenwood, 1969); Robert Griffith, *The Politics of Fear: Joseph R. McCarthy and the Senate* (Lexington: University Press of Kentucky, 1970); Athan G. Theoharis, *Seeds of Repression: Harry S. Truman and the Origins of McCarthyism* (Chicago: Quadrangle, 1971); the same writer and Robert Griffith, eds., *The Specter: Original Essays on the Cold War and the Origins of McCarthyism* (New York: New Viewpoints, 1974); Lewis McCarroll Purifoy, *Harry Truman's China Policy: McCarthyism and the Diplomacy of Hysteria, 1947–1951* (New York: New Viewpoints, 1976).

A miscellany of titles are Stephen Hess, *Organizing the Presidency* (Washington: The Brookings Institution, 1976), on the White House and executive office staffs; Francis H. Heller, ed., *The Truman White House: The Administration of the Presidency, 1945–1953* (Lawrence: Regents

Press of Kansas, 1980); Ken Hechler, *Working with Truman* (New York: Putnam, 1982), by a White House staffer (as was Hess); Ronald T. Farrar, *Reluctant Servant: The Story of Charles G. Ross* (Columbia: University of Missouri Press, 1969); Edward Hughes Pruden, *A Window on Washington* (New York: Vantage, 1976), by the pastor of the First Baptist Church; Edward S. Flash, Jr., *Economic Advice and Presidential Leadership: The Council of Economic Advisers* (New York: Columbia University Press, 1965); Francis H. Heller, ed., *Economics and the Truman Administration* (Lawrence: Regents Press of Kansas, 1981); Athan G. Theoharis, *The Truman Presidency: The Origins of the Imperial Presidency and the National Security State* (New York: Coleman, 1979); Steve Neal, "Our Best and Worst Presidents," *Chicago Tribune Magazine*, Jan. 10, 1982.

Index

96595

9659

ISBN 0-673-39337-2